Something GAINED

7 Shifts to Be
STRONGER, SMARTER & HAPPIER
After Divorce

Deb Purdy

InsightSTREAM

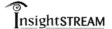
Cover design by www.CreativeShoebox.com

Book design by www.JustYourType.biz

ISBN-978-0-9979589-0-4

For Sophie and Tess:

Being your mom is one of the great joys of my life. I'm grateful for you two every day. You continue to amaze and inspire me.

Table of Contents

Chapter 1

Choosing to Shift: Can this book really help me? 1

Anatomy of a Shift—From Information to Transformation 2

I've Been There Too 5

It Got Messy Fast 7

Everything Must Change for Everything to Change 8

And You Can Too 11

How This Book Is Organized 12

Chapter 2

Culture Shift: Not all marriages are meant to last, and that's OK 15

Why Do "I Do"? 16

No-Shame, No-Blame Reframe 18

Shifty Action Step 1: Rate Your Starting Point, Measure Your Progress 20

Shifty Action Step 2: Ask for Help If You Need It 22

Quick Lift 1: Just Breathe! 23

Quick Lift 2: Rock On 23

Chapter 3

Shift Your Intentions: What you focus on is what you get 25

Your Personal Super Powers 29

Living on Purpose 32

Shifty Action Step 3: Creating Powerful Divorce (or Breakup) Intentions .. 36

Quick Lift 3: Good News Diet 40

Chapter 4

Shift Your Story: You are the hero of your own story **43**

Is Your Story Holding You Back?..45

Attachment-to-Freedom Scale..48

Destructive Divorce Storylines..49

Shifty Action Step 4: Gifts and Blessings Inventory 54

Shifty Action Step 5: Active Self-Compassion 57

Quick Lift 4: Create an "Advisory Board" of Personal Heroes......61

Chapter 5

Shift on Your Ex: Can't we all just get along? **63**

Decide What You Want 65

But, What If My Ex Is a #$@&%*!? 67

Create Your Vision..71

An Invitation to Accelerate Your Results 76

Divorce Vows..77

Shifty Action Step 6: Let It OUT 80

Shifty Action Step 7: Is It Time to Use the "F" Word? 82

Quick Lift 5: Joy to the World!..86

Chapter 6

Shift the Conversation: Teach people how to support you **91**

Changing the Conversation with Yourself....................................93

Changing the Conversation with Others......................................96

Shifty Action Step 8: Time Traveling for 30 Seconds a Day 99

Shifty Action Step 9: Know What You Want (and What You Don't)..........100

Quick Lift 6: Seven Minutes in Heaven......................................104

Chapter 7

Kids Are Shifters Too!: Help your kids thrive after divorce 107

Let Them Talk, Let Them Cry 108

Don't Practice Poison Parenting 110

Co-Create Your New Normal 112

Get Busy Healing Yourself... 114

Shifty Action Step 10: Meeting of the Hearts and Minds 115

Quick Lift 7: What I Like About You.. 116

Chapter 8

Shift On: Your divorce is a life "Do-Over" 119

Taking Care of Future "You".. 121

I Have a Dream.. 123

Finding the Extraordinary in the Ordinary............................... 125

Shifty Action Step 11: Inside-Out Goal Setting........................ 127

Shifty Action Step 12: From the Future with Love.................... 132

Quick Lift 8: Daydream Believer 134

Quick Lift 9: Kind Is the New Happy.. 135

A Final Word.. 137

About the Author 139

Acknowledgments 141

CHAPTER 1

Choosing to Shift:
Can this book really help me?

I bet you didn't plan on your relationship going up in flames. I didn't. I felt certain that my marriage would land squarely on the correct side of the 50 percent divorce rate. I was smug about it. On the day we got married in 1995, we were mid-thirty-somethings with established careers, mutual long-term goals and crackling chemistry. We were ready. We were in love. What could go wrong? Just about everything it turns out. But more about that in a minute.

First, you want to know, can this book really help *me*? That depends on your willingness to do one thing…the single most important thing that will determine whether, and how fast, you'll recover, heal and thrive after your divorce or breakup. It's simply this: know that you have a choice, and then make a decision to use your divorce or breakup experience to your advantage. That means you'll use it to learn, grow and evolve—not only to move through and out of pain, but to move into the life you want for yourself.

"How do I do that?" you might ask. You're in exactly the right place to get answers; this book will show you how. But everything happens in the context of this first decision. I'm inviting you to accept that you can use this experience as something that happened "for" you, not "to" you. It's a much more powerful position from which to move forward. To succeed, all you have to do is be open to this idea, even if you're not quite feeling it right now. Everything else from here on is the instruction manual.

If you're in, let's get started!

First, I want to congratulate you on opening yourself up to reinventing what your divorce means to you. This is a very self-honoring action. I assume you're reading this because, quite simply, you intend to thrive and you're supporting yourself in that. I acknowledge you for taking a proactive role in creating your life the way you want it. I wrote this book for you.

Anatomy of a Shift—From Information to Transformation

A shift is a fundamental change in perspective. It has stages. A stage-one shift occurs when you become aware of a new idea or concept and it sounds true. You intuitively know that it could make a difference in your life but you may not be sure how. At this stage, shifts are slippery. It's very easy to hear something that's potentially important to you, feel the truth of it and go right back to business as usual.

For example, I recently saw a video on social media about a 90-something-year-old woman who is a yoga instructor and lives her life fully every day. I felt so inspired by her attitude and message that I shared it with my friends. It sparked a deep recognition inside of me. It opened me up to the idea that aging doesn't have to be a slow march to decrepitude in body, mind and spirit. Then, I dove back into my day and forgot about it.

In stage two, you grab the shift and work a little harder to incorporate it into your life. For instance, you may print out an inspirational quote, or read a book, that puts the idea into words. You more intentionally remind yourself of it but you're not quite "living it" yet. They say that in advertising, you have to hear a message seven times for it to stick with you. In a way, shifts are similar.

> ❝ Sometimes, you're reminded of something you've heard before, but suddenly, you really "get it." It changes you on the cellular level and begins to inform your thoughts, feelings and actions. ❞

I was reminded about the yoga video when I saw another social media post about a 75-year-old who celebrated her birthday by skydiving for the first time. The shift started to get a foothold. Aging can be more interesting than I had previously imagined. I bought a book on healthy aging and started to take proactive steps to keep my body and mind healthy. The shift was gaining some traction.

Sometimes, you're reminded of something you've heard before, but suddenly, you really "get it." That's a stage-three shift. The information lands deeply inside of you as something you really and truly know. It changes you on the cellular level and begins to inform your thoughts, feelings and actions. It has a true impact on your life.

My stage-three shift about aging happened during a workshop when I was asked to write a vision for what my old age would look like. As I began to write, I became very intentional about my plan for myself to have a fun-filled and vital last chapter. The shift landed deeply inside of me at that moment and made a fundamental change in how I think about my own aging—from fear and dread to embracing and accepting.

In this book, I'm going to introduce you to (or remind you of) seven key shifts that give you the power to view your relationship and divorce with gratitude and peace. The book combines the content and exercises you need to move from information to transformation— from stage one, knowing about the shift, to stage three, living the shift.

Healing Happens in Layers. Everyone reading this book is at a different stage. You could be newly separated and in the grip of the raw pain, stress and fear that come with the death of a relationship as you knew it. In that case, this book may serve as a beacon of hope for what awaits you on the other side of this experience. It can also be a guide for how to navigate your way through this experience with more intention and personal power.

Or, the heart-rending emotional chaos from when your divorce or breakup was new could be a fading memory. But, months or years after the fact, you still feel lingering anger or guilt. Maybe you get a negative "charge" when it comes to your Ex, and that easily tips you into bitter reminiscences. You sense your healing is unfinished on some indefinable level. It's over, but you're not over it. In that case, this book will help you move into peace and acceptance.

You owe it to yourself to use every experience to enhance your life, even your divorce.

I've Been There Too

My story is no different than many others. A series of disappointments built on miscommunications built on resentments. Needs went unmet. Words went unsaid. Who was this a-hole and why did he feel so completely different about so many of the fundamental aspects of what makes a happy marriage?

We didn't agree about money. We didn't agree about sex. We couldn't even agree on how to fight. Our conflicting "talk it out right now" and "silent brooding for days" styles didn't bode well for our success rate in negotiating and compromising. What I didn't know then that I know now is that we had very different but inter-related patterns of behavior that were largely automatic and unconscious. His default reaction was to get over-the-top mad about the smallest things. A normally very nice and amiable guy, he had a current of unaddressed anger right under the surface that was very easily triggered. My knee-jerk pattern was to "over-please" in an effort to keep everything harmonious. I had a deep and unaddressed fear of anger. He would get mad and withdraw. I would frantically bend over backwards to smooth things over. You see where this is going.

Flash forward 10 years and two kids. We were basically angry, squabbling roommates, and I was truly miserable. Yet, I felt like I couldn't leave—I had made this bed and put two kids in it. I had to lie in it or die trying. There was no infidelity on either side, but we were living separate emotional lives. Then, in the summer of 2005, we took a family vacation to San Diego. He and I and our two young children in a hotel room together for a week.

Match, meet dynamite. On about the third morning, I snapped at him for reading the paper while I struggled to wrangle the kids. He snapped back. Things escalated and he refused to go on our planned excursion to the zoo. I remember the huge lump in my throat as I took the kids to breakfast on my own. I was awash in unexpressed and impotent rage—a feeling with which I was all too familiar. As the girls chattered about the upcoming day, my eyes suddenly focused on a brick wall that was facing our table in the diner. I had an instant epiphany. I. Am. Done. Kaboom.

It Got Messy Fast

You don't know what awkward is until you've spent a week on vacation with a person you've decided to leave after 10 years of marriage. I told him within a few days of getting home and, shockingly, he was blindsided. He had no idea and that made it even worse. People asked me if we tried counseling. We didn't. When we first married, he told me he'd had a very bad experience with a past therapist and he didn't trust that method of personal growth. At the time, I didn't think we would ever need it. So naïve!

Thinking back, I can understand his reaction to my sudden announcement. Up until I made that instant decision in the diner, I didn't think I could ever leave. He was sticking to our tacit agreement to stay together for the kids. I simply "hit the wall" and could not keep it up. We both had our case for what led to our split. There was a lot of blame and anger on both sides. We both firmly positioned ourselves as the victim.

That was the beginning of a very dark time. My attorney, referred by a friend of a friend, was a cynical cliché. He sized me up after 10 minutes on the phone and put my Ex and me into a category he'd seen a million times—dominant husband and acquiescent wife. He was controlling and I was controlled. My attorney proceeded accordingly. Everything he said about my soon-to-be ex-husband was derogatory and inflammatory.

Our dueling attorneys coached us to go for the gusto

without any consideration of salvaging the long-term relationship. It was a get-what-you-can, survival-of-the-fittest free-for-all. My family and friends joined in the judging fest. So did his. We were both validated and vindicated by our loyal supporters.

Our conversations were upsetting, unsettling and hostile. My body would flood with stress whenever I saw his name come up on my phone. I would steel myself for another onslaught. Every encounter left me drained, angry and feeling vaguely like I was losing the war. I could not think about him, talk about him or talk to him without feeling overwhelmingly negative.

For someone afraid of anger directed toward her, an ugly divorce was my worst nightmare. I was walking straight through hell with no end in sight as we bitterly argued over the details. I felt incredibly guilty about what all of this free-flowing hostility was doing to my eight- and five-year-old girls. Since they were so young, it wouldn't be truly "over" when it was over. After one particularly brutal phone call, I realized with mounting horror that I had many more years of having to deal with him as their other parent.

Everything Must Change for Everything to Change

On top of everything else, I was freaked out about what I was going to do with my life. I'd spent most of my career as a professional communicator in the corporate world. I had quit the year before the divorce to start my own creative business, which was not all I hoped it would be. At that point, "Exy" and I were unable to come to agreeable terms. We were poised to sit on either side of a conference table, flanked by our take-no-prisoners attorneys. In short, everything was a mess.

Then, a light emerged from the darkness. I had acted as a life coach for my friends for as long as I could remember. I felt strongly called to formalize this gift into a career. But I knew I had to get my act together first. Despite the complexity of my home life, I enrolled in a master's degree program in Spiritual Psychology at the University of Santa Monica (USM). Spiritual Psychology at USM is defined as "the study and practice of the art and science of Conscious Awakening." At USM, I learned to transform life experiences into opportunities to experience a greater connection with who I really am as a loving, peaceful, compassionate and joyful being.

When I signed up, I thought I would be learning to help others, and I did. But, even more significantly, the program was personally transformational on every level. I quickly learned it was possible to transcend my story and look at my life from a higher altitude. I realized that as long as I wallowed in the who-did-what-to-whom world, I could not look at my Ex in any other way than as my persecutor and myself as his victim. As long as I was in that frame of mind, I had no power to change anything. Even worse, I was likely to unconsciously seek out another "persecutor" for my next partner. Ugh!

Fortunately, I had these insights days before our

scheduled attorney-driven showdown. In a moment of clarity, I realized the objective for both parties was to prevail—a narrowly focused, short-term goal. Recognizing that yes, I wanted a fair agreement in the short term, I thought, "What's my real goal?" I began to realize that, if at all possible, I also wanted to have a positive, friendly and peaceful relationship with the father of my children, with whom I had many years of parenting left.

I decided right then that he and I had to work this out in a way that would start to rebuild, not tear down, our bond. This goal became more important to me than holding on so tightly to being the victim. By making the shift, I opened up the space in myself to see more clearly and get creative about ways to compromise. When he saw that I was approaching him from a new, more open-hearted angle, he too was able to bend. I saw that he was willing to find a way to bridge the gap. We were able to go back to our respective attorneys and make our agreement with a more collaborative approach.

With that, he and I laid a foundation of trust that has served me well as we have worked through conflicts in the ensuing years. As I continued to learn and shift, something miraculous happened. He also spontaneously shifted. He could intuitively sense that I had let go of judging him and started taking responsibility for my contribution to our dysfunctional marriage patterns. Over time, this freed him to let down his guard and work with me.

Ironically, thanks to what I learned in my master's program, we were working through issues better than we ever had during our marriage. We went from deeply hostile and just plain nasty to civil, then to friendly and now relaxed.

And You Can Too

While in the depths of my own divorce, I had a revelation. It dawned on me that my marriage and divorce experience was providing me with all of the raw materials to reinvent my life for the better. I was getting a "do over;" only now, I had more wisdom and experience to work with.

I made a shift. I went out of victim mode and took back ownership of my life. I decided to use my marriage and divorce experience as a learning lab. I decided to examine what I really wanted for myself and what I needed to do or change to get it. And, for the good of my girls, I set my intention to reinvent my relationship with my Ex from adversarial to collaborative co-parents.

❝ While in the depths of my own divorce, I had a revelation. I was getting a "do over;" only now, I had more wisdom and experience to work with. ❞

Today, my Ex and I work together cooperatively and our kids are reaping the benefit. Best of all, I'm not only at peace when it comes to my divorce, but I'm also grateful for all that I gained from the experience. The process I went through was so powerful and transformational that I felt called to put it out there to help others.

You have a fundamental choice about how you want

to use your divorce. In fact, as I mentioned in the beginning, recognizing the fact that you have a choice lays the foundation for your first shift. Breaking up may not be what you would have chosen for yourself or your family, but it's your reality and you have the opportunity to use it to make your life better.

You can do this. You just need to want to. I'll tell you how.

How This Book Is Organized

My intention for this book is to help you use your breakup or divorce as a springboard to create the life you want. My process, outlined for you here, is really a series of small, intentional changes in your inner landscape that I refer to as "shifts" that build on each other.

The book is divided into sections that outline and explain the seven essential shifts:

Culture Shift—Transforming your relationship to divorce itself

Shift Your Intentions—Setting powerful intentions to improve your inner and outer life

Shift Your Story—Breaking free from the three most common destructive post-divorce story lines

Shift on Your Ex—Transforming anger, blame and fear into peace, acceptance and personal power

Shift the Conversation—Teaching your friends and family how to best support you as you recover and heal

Kids Are Shifters Too!—What to do and what not to do as you help your kids recover and thrive after your divorce

Shift On—Reinventing your life after divorce

As you go through the book, you will build your shifting muscle step-by-step. Included in each chapter, you'll find "Shifty Action Steps" to help you anchor and deepen your shifts. And, because along with these longer-term shifts it's important to get a little instant gratification, I've included "Quick Lifts" you can use to instantly lift and lighten your mood and your heart.

I suggest that you revisit sections that really hit home with you, maybe even redo some of the steps, to take yourself to a deeper level. This is a living process that will deepen each time you do it.

By the way, I use the words divorce and breakup interchangeably. The information I provide applies to thriving after the end of any committed relationship, regardless of whether or not you were married.

If any clinical depression, spousal abuse, substance abuse or criminal activity occurred during your marriage or divorce, please also seek out support from a professional who is specially trained to assist you with your specific issue.

CHAPTER 2

Culture Shift: Not all marriages are meant to last, and that's OK

"I'm sorry."

Expressed with a pained look of sympathy, this is the universal response to the news of divorce. Often followed by "Did you try counseling?" or "Wasn't there any way you could have worked it out?" Yes, I did get those intrusive, not to mention judgmental, questions. I'm sure you have, too.

They mean well. However, inquiries like these point to the general cultural consensus that something has gone terribly wrong. The marriage has failed. And, by extension, in some fundamental way, so have the two people involved. Divorce is not considered a good outcome. This belief is so deeply embedded in our modern culture that we rarely question it.

The truth is not all marriages are meant to last a life-time. How do we know this? Because almost half of them don't. A life-long, happy marriage is wonderful to behold and something to which we can aspire. However, it's not the only standard by which to measure relationship "success."

A union of any life span, whether it's six months or twenty-five years, offers many gifts and blessings for both parties. Here's the thing; if we use the experience to grow as a person, although the outcome is different, it's no less important or successful than a life-long marriage. The first thing we need to do to start making the shift about the definition of a successful marriage is to reexamine the purpose of a marriage.

Why Do "I Do"?

Far from being static and traditional, the purpose for and meaning of marriage have evolved along with human-kind. Through most of the history of Western civilization, marriage has been more about money, property, politics and survival than about love or personal choice. In this context, romantic love was not a primary, or even second-ary, reason for a match. It was not until the Victorian era that the idea of married love gained some traction. Even then, it wasn't the most important consideration.

Starting in the twentieth century, love emerged as a legitimate reason for marriage. In the 1950s, marriage became ubiquitous. Society looked askance at those who remained single and social acceptance was the primary motivation for many unions. The 60s and 70s brought changing social mores. Quarreling couples, who had married for love, split up rather than stay together, and the divorce rate rose accordingly.

In our modern-day relationship mythology, our marriage partners should be funny, sensitive and attractive best friends who contribute financially, are amazing in bed and know what we want before we do. Thanks chick flicks. The fantasy of a perfect wedding followed by "happily ever after" has put pressure on the modern marriage that it can't support. There exists an unspoken expectation that by marrying, we will finally obtain true love and happiness.

> ❝The fantasy of a perfect wedding followed by 'happily ever after' has put pressure on the modern marriage that it can't support.❞

Things will be better. Our problems will be solved. At no point in human history has a marriage been expected to meet such extraordinary expectations. This gap between what we want and what we can reasonably expect from another person is immense.

But there exists a deeper-seated relationship saboteur that's much closer to home. Many of us look to our partners to fulfill unmet needs that we don't even understand ourselves. Would you let a child decide who you will marry? Of course not, right? But, you probably did just that. Often, our relationships act as mirrors reflecting our childhood wounds back to us. For example, being continually let down by a parent who was too busy to, or didn't know how to, connect emotionally could result in difficulty trusting or a fear of abandonment that plays out under the surface of a marriage.

Many people go into relationships with the unconscious expectation that the other person can heal us where we were hurt as children. This unconscious desire to have our partners fill the needs left behind by our all-too-human parents is often the root cause of the battles and eventual breakdown of relationships.

No-Shame, No-Blame Reframe

So, what's left for us to do? Intentionally acknowledge one of the most important but under-appreciated dimensions of modern relationships—their value as the perfect laboratory for personal growth. We can use relationships, both past and present, to learn about ourselves and heal. Rather than expecting our partners to make us whole, we begin to find our own wholeness.

In reevaluating what marriage means to us individually, to our families and culturally, we are also reframing divorce. Let's shift from moralizing about and lamenting divorce to understanding that a successful marriage, no matter the length, is one that contributes to knowing ourselves better and evolving into more loving and compassionate people.

The "No-Shame, No-Blame Reframe" is a new, more loving and self-supportive way of looking at marriage and divorce. You can begin to see that by letting go of the narrow-minded view that divorce = failure, the experience can be valuable to all involved. When you operate from this open-hearted approach, the blessings and lessons of your relationship are more readily available to you. Even your kids can benefit if you make the choice to model for them what it looks like to face change with an open heart and an open mind. Viewed through this lens, you can decide to release any lingering sense of shame.

❝ Let's shift from moralizing about and lamenting divorce to understanding that a successful marriage, no matter the length, is one that contributes to knowing ourselves better and evolving into more loving and compassionate people. ❞

Let's also acknowledge our collective bravery for putting ourselves out there in the first place. It takes guts and a certain amount of optimism to commit to another person. The reality is that divorce is not good or bad, it just is. Shame, blame and judgment shut you down. Reframing divorce as a catalyst you can use to know yourself better, heal your wounds and improve your life opens you up to reaping the gifts that are inherent in the experience.

SHIFTY ACTION STEP (SAS)

Shifty Action Steps are tools to help you deepen and integrate the Seven Shifts into your life.

♥ SAS 1: Rate Your Starting Point, Measure Your Progress

Without question, divorce is one of life's most difficult and stressful experiences. Residual negative feelings can linger for months, or even years, after the fact. To support yourself in this shift, and the ones to follow, it's very useful to see where you're starting.

Knowing that things can change from day to day, use the Reframing Rating Scale below to observe and rate your current predominant state of mind when it comes to your divorce or breakup. Then, see the corresponding Reframing Statement. You can use these statements to help gradually deliver yourself into a newer and more self-supportive mindset.

Continue to review the chart as you progress through the book. Once you've completed the book, measure your progress up the chart. This isn't a race or a reason to judge yourself. Everyone's on their own timetable and there's no right or wrong. This is simply a way to see where you're starting. You can use it to see how you continue to evolve over time with the help of this or any other book, course, coaching or therapy.

Reframing Rating Scale

Rating Scale	State of Mind	Reframing Statement
9-10: Thrive	Love and gratitude are constantly present inside of me, regardless of what's happening on the outside. I find great joy in proactively creating my life the way I want it.	I'm grateful for everything that happens in my life and use all of my experiences for personal growth. My decisions are guided by my vision and intention for my life. While, like everyone, I have an occasional bad day or down period, overall, I'm optimistic and feel good about my life.
7-8: Enjoy	I'm actively using my past experiences as information to grow; I see my challenges as opportunities. I'm excited about what's next.	Even though life isn't perfect, I know how to work with myself to find the gifts and blessings in every experience. I acknowledge that I have some power over how I feel. I'm willing to take responsibility for nurturing my optimism by taking positive, self-supporting actions.
5-6: Engage	I see the value in using my past experiences to grow. I'm intentional about making positive changes; I'm optimistic about what's next.	Even though I still have many hard days, I'm supporting myself in making positive changes. I've decided that I'm willing to seek out, learn and apply ideas for how to feel better. I acknowledge that I'm in a process that actively helps me feel more optimistic.
3-4: Persevere	I'm hanging in there and feel I'm doing pretty well in spite of all that's happened. Sometimes, I feel stuck, but sometimes, I see a glimmer of hope for change.	Even though I'm not yet where I want to be and I'm not feeling particularly optimistic, I'm willing to acknowledge that I can feel better. Even though I don't know how it will come about, I'm willing to decide that I will feel better at some point.
2: Endure	I feel like my options are limited. I'm often anxious, sad and/or mad and I'm uncertain about how to change that. I feel stuck.	Even though it seems like I'm always going to feel this way and right now I doubt things can change, I'm willing to acknowledge that there's a possibility that I can feel better. Even though I don't know how it will come about, I'm willing to allow myself to feel better.

(Continued on next page)

Rating Scale	State of Mind	Reframing Statement
1: Survive	Anger, grief, blame and/or fear are constantly present. Life is hard and I've had bad luck in relationships. I feel powerless to change.	Even though I'm miserable right now and feel that there's no way out, I'm willing to begin to acknowledge that there's a possibility that I can feel better. Even though I don't know how it will come about, I'm willing to open myself to that possibility.

Visit www.DebPurdy.com/resources for a PDF of the Reframing Rating Scale.

SAS 2: Ask for Help If You Need It

Your relationship has given you a great gift. It's a rich source of valuable information about your unconscious patterns and childhood wounds. With this awareness comes the choice to break out of the programs that are running through all of your relationships, romantic or otherwise. Whether you choose to partner up again or live happily solo, delving into this area of self-awareness is very important work—and is out of the scope of this book. If this is a challenge for you, I recommend *Conscious Loving* by Gay and Kathlyn Hendricks, an excellent book that can help you start to identify your patterns and heal old wounds. Remember, you don't have to do everything by yourself. If you feel stuck or overwhelmed, ask for help from a coach or therapist.

Quick Lifts (QL)

When you're navigating a big life transition, your mood can change on a minute-by-minute basis. Sometimes, it seems like a mood gets ahold of you and you're along for the ride until it lets you go. However, there are real, pro-active steps you can take to get some immediate relief as you work through your bigger shifts.

▪ *QL 1: Just Breathe!*

When you notice that you are in the grip of thoughts that make you feel bad and stress you out, get an instant mini-shift with some quick breath work. To start, inhale deeply for a count of four (feel your chest and belly expand), then exhale for a count of four (all through the nose, which adds a natural resistance to the breath). Repeat this three to five times. While you are doing this, it's important to clear your mind by putting your focus completely on your breath moving into, and then slowly out of, your body. Aim to work your way up to six to eight counts per breath with the same goal in mind: Calm the nervous system, in-crease focus, reduce stress and take your mind off racing or distracting negative thoughts. Repeat as needed!

▪ *QL 2: Rock On*

Music is magical when it comes to changing or lifting a mood. In fact, scientists at the University of Missouri have found that people can boost their mood simply by listening to upbeat music. Support yourself by putting together a playlist of songs that lift your spirits—listen to it daily. From current toe-tappers to rousing classical, it's a great eye-opener first thing in the morning. Or, keep your favorite song on stand-by for a boost during the day. You can supercharge your mini-shift by dancing around like no one is watching. Relax your way to sleep with sounds of nature, wind chimes or soothing music.

Summary

This chapter discussed the first shift: transforming your relationship to divorce. It invited you to release feelings of failure, shame, blame, guilt and other negative feelings associated with divorce. It introduced the idea of using your marriage as a personal growth laboratory by identifying unhealed childhood wounds and unconscious relationship patterns so you don't have to repeat them in your next partnership. It reframed divorce as a catalyst for proactively reinventing your life in a way that brings you more love, peace and joy.

CHAPTER 3

Shift Your Intentions:
What you focus on is what you get

Did you know that how you think about your divorce has more impact on your experience than any outside person or issue? That's because your thoughts create your personal reality. When you examine them, you'll notice that your thoughts come in waves of similar and corresponding thoughts. They build on each other. If your stream of thoughts is strongly negative (or positive), that generates emotions. Emotions give your thoughts more power.

When you're feeling strong emotions, you bring your thoughts further into reality by talking about them. Then you make choices—take action—based on them. Your thoughts impact how you feel, what you believe and what you do or don't do. You create your reality with every choice you make, and your choices are based on your predominant thoughts. In a very real way, your inner world shapes your outer one.

You see this when two people experience the exact same thing but have very different responses. My friend Judy is truly able to put her focus on the possibilities of every experience. She recently attended a parent-teacher conference for her second-grade son. She walked out of the meeting brimming with enthusiasm for the young teacher's energy and fresh ideas. Her Ex, Tom, walked out of the same meeting lamenting what he saw as the decline of the educational system embodied by this inexperienced new teacher.

Same experience, different inner world. Who's right? I don't know about you, but I would rather live in Judy's world. We evolved to evaluate threats. It's in our nature to look for what could go wrong in order to keep ourselves safe. But this often has the opposite effect when our lens on the world keeps us feeling perpetually unsafe. Or, in Tom's case, disgruntled, worried and unsatisfied.

❝ Your thoughts create your world and yet, if you're like most people, you barely pay attention to them. Here's a liberating idea: you don't have to believe everything you think. ❞

Your thoughts create your world and yet, if you're like most people, you barely pay attention to them. Here's a liberating idea: you don't have to believe everything you think. In fact, when you observe your thoughts, you can question them. When a stream of negative thoughts gets a foothold in your mind, acknowledge it. Ask yourself these questions:

- What if it's not true?
- Is it possible there's a different perspective I'm not considering?
- What are three other ways I could interpret this?

When you observe your thoughts, you can begin noticing how many negative thoughts you entertain in a day and how much they affect your actions and emotions. Then, decide if you want to choose thoughts that feel better. This isn't about trying to force positive thinking when you don't feel it. It's about noticing and acknowledging negative thinking and then simply questioning it.

My client, Chloe, married her high school sweetheart at 18 and was divorced at 55. She had devoted most of her adult life to raising her family and taking care of her home. When her husband left her for a business associate, she felt totally powerless.

She had married with the idea that he was going to take care of her. Now that the marriage was over, she had to figure out a way to take care of herself. At first, her thoughts about her future prospects were steeped in fear and hopelessness. Variations of "I don't have any skills or experience" and "No one will ever hire me" churned through her mind. As long as she kept these thoughts front and center, she was paralyzed and overwhelmed.

She could not move forward.

In the middle of one of her darkest nights, her mind was busy working its way through her litany of worries. She was so stressed that she knew she had to find a new approach. During our session the next day, I had her write all of her worries down one by one. Then, right next to each worry statement, I asked her to write out opposite statements. So, next to "What if I can't find a job that pays me enough money?" she wrote "What if I found my dream job paying me more than enough?"

We asked the question, "Why is the negative 'What if' any more valid than the positive one?" The first thing she noticed was that just by entertaining the possibility that her thoughts were not necessarily TRUE, she was relieved of some stress. She decided to make a habit of catching her worry thoughts and playing what she started calling the "opposites game."

Even though she didn't often completely believe the opposite thought was true either, she started to open up to the fact that there might be something in-between that she could live with. She started paying attention to her thoughts throughout the day and asking the opposite "What if?" question when her worries threatened to take hold. Doing this opened up a space inside her to see past her worries to her possibilities.

One day soon after, her best friend asked her to help pick out a couch and that sparked an idea. She had a good eye and her friends were always asking her to help them decorate. She realized that she really loved doing that.

New thoughts started to take hold. Now, instead of dwelling on and talking about what she had previously perceived as her insurmountable obstacles, she slowly started shifting her focus to new possibilities.

Though still scared, she completed a three-month interior design certificate program at night. Eventually, she partnered with a real estate broker to help home sellers "stage" their homes for sale. Five years later, she makes a great living collaborating with several real estate agents and she's never been happier. She got her power back and transformed her life using the tools we're going to talk about next.

Your Personal Super Powers

Yes, we all have super powers! By that, I mean everyone comes standardly equipped with the internal resources necessary to make the kind of transformation that Chloe did—from hopeless, to optimistic, to joyful. Until now, you might not have been aware of your powers. That doesn't mean you haven't been using them. You have. You've just been using them on the default settings. That is, up to this point, they have been deploying based on your predominant unexamined thoughts. How do you know if this is true? Look around. If your life is short of what your dreams are for yourself, you have an opportunity to explore using your super powers on purpose.

Your first super power is awareness—knowing that "today's you" has tremendous power to make things better for "future you." This is a simple, but very exciting, concept. What's new about this idea is using it in this moment. That means understanding that your life, right this minute, is the culmination of your past beliefs, feelings, thoughts and actions. All of your power is RIGHT NOW. What you believe, think and do now has more impact on your future reality than anything in your past.

Doing things for yourself now takes care of you both now and later. You can enjoy the current moment for what it is while also setting future you up for more joy. Awareness is powerful because it's the gateway into choice, your next super power. It's an essential ingredient of change. It's the awareness that you have the power to create something different for yourself if you choose to, starting now.

❝ What's in your past doesn't matter. Neither does what you plan to do at some future time. What matters is what you do with this moment. It's making the conscious choice to use this very minute to move you closer to what you want in your life. ❞

What's in your past doesn't matter. Neither does what you plan to do at some future time. What matters is what you do with this moment. It's making the conscious choice to use this very minute to move you closer to what you want in your life. There is no in-between.

Recently divorced and feeling a little stuck, my client Ken got intrigued by this idea. He worked in a job that he didn't enjoy and the days were flying by without him making any forward motion toward his dreams. He didn't know what to do so he did nothing. Today's Ken was setting future Ken up for more of the same.

As we worked together, he started to become more aware that doing nothing was actually decision by indecision. He was making a passive choice, but it was a choice just the same. It hit home with him that, whether he did anything about it or not, he did have choices. Once that awareness took root, he made the decision to put some of his focus on exploring his options (which, coincidently, is the next super power).

You can have awareness, but unless you're willing to direct some of your focus and attention to what you want, you'll stay where you are. So, focus works hand in hand with awareness and choice. (Your time reading this book is a great example of putting your focus on what you want to create next for yourself.)

A stressed-out single mom, Sienna was pretty clear that she wanted to feel more calm and peaceful. After doing some research, she decided that trying meditation might be beneficial. Her biggest issue was time. When we started working together, her two kids and full-time job kept her very busy. I really understood her situation. And, I still felt that she could find some time to focus on what she wanted.

When we looked at her schedule, it became clear she was using binge-watching TV and internet surfing to try and de-stress after her kids went to bed. Unfortunately, this strategy left her more tired, a little depressed and just as stressed. She committed to carving out five minutes a night, before she started on TV, to try a guided meditation. She found it very relaxing and it soon became a habit.

After a few weeks, she started supplementing her evening meditation by reading a few pages of an uplifting book instead of automatically turning to TV. Now, a year later, she still has TV shows she likes, and that's fine. But, she watches a show or two and then turns off the set. She still meditates and she's found a deep reserve of calm she never knew she had, all because she was willing to shift some of her focus to what she wanted to create for herself.

Like Sienna, you are creating your life moment by moment. You're aware you have the choice to change things for yourself starting this minute. You're willing to focus your attention on doing it.

The next super power, intention, is about directing the first three powers toward what you want. Intentions are proactive decisions about how you're going to "show up"—inside yourself and outside in the world. Your intentions lead to inspired thoughts and actions that create forward momentum toward what you want.

Living on Purpose

Intention-setting is not about dogged determination or forcing yourself to succeed at all costs. It's the process of deciding what it is you want and getting a clear picture of it. It's your intentions that determine the direction you're headed and, ultimately, the results you get. Without clear intentions, we tend to roll from one situation we don't like to another we don't like. Our lives become more about avoidance than conscious creation. Intentions give you purpose.

So, what does all of this have to do with your divorce or breakup? Good question! Without a doubt, setting intentions is a powerful tool for both inner peace and outer results in any part of your life. However, for our purposes, we're going to focus on setting post-divorce intentions. So, let's start with a few guidelines.

Be positive and affirming—Your intentions should say what you want, not what you don't want. For example:

- Weak Intention: My intention is not to get angry or anxious when I meet with my Ex.

- Powerful Intention: I intend to breathe deeply to help me relax and to calmly hold my boundaries when I meet with my Ex.

Assume success—Don't build qualifiers into your intentions. For example:

- Weak Intention: My intention is to remain peaceful inside myself when my Ex picks up the kids, as long as he's on time.
- Powerful Intention: My intention is to remain peaceful inside myself when my Ex picks up the kids.

Come from your values and beliefs— Strive to get in touch with the deepest and truest part of yourself and set your intentions from that place.

After his second wife moved out, Ken was deeply hurt and full of anger. How could this have happened again? After the worst of the shock wore off, he decided to use the experience to grow as a person. He realized that after his first marriage ended, he had jumped fairly quickly into dating without much reflection. Being single was uncomfortable for him and he fell into the relationship that became his second marriage.

With two divorces under his belt, Ken set his intention to learn about his own unconscious relationship patterns. He also set his intention to move from judgment and bitterness to forgiveness and acceptance. His sister, who was his closest confidant, was still very angry and didn't understand his desire to move past the rage. Thankfully, Ken was true to himself and based his intentions on his own inner guidance rather than his sister's influence.

It paid off. With the help of a therapist, he learned about his unconscious need for approval that led to him marrying two women with many of the same characteristics. Armed with this self-knowledge, he made a list of requirements for the qualities he wanted in a life partner. Three years later, he's in a committed relationship with someone who's a great fit for him.

Another one of my clients, Barb, had an Ex who was habitually late picking up their kids. As the agreed-on time came and went, she could feel herself becoming very worked up. By the time he arrived, she would be upset and so would the kids. This inevitably started a nasty scene. She realized this amount of stress wasn't good for her or her kids and she set the intention to let go of taking it personally. Her Ex had always been looser about the definition of "on time" than she was. And, maybe it really was a passive-aggressive move on his part. So what? She couldn't control how he conducted his life. What she could control was how she responded. Her next intention was to transform waiting into action.

If she didn't have somewhere else to be at the scheduled pick-up time, her chosen action was to just let it go. That by itself was liberating. In the most practical sense, it had little impact on her if her kids were playing in their rooms waiting for their dad while she zoomed through her household to-do list or relaxed with a magazine. If she did have plans, she came up with another strategy. She often took the kids with her, letting her Ex know where to pick them up. So, instead of putting off running errands until he got there, she took the kids along. Many times, he would show up halfway through a grocery shopping trip and take them from there. Or, in the instances when taking them along wasn't possible, she dropped them with a neighbor to keep an eye on them until he arrived.

At first, her friends thought she was crazy for what they perceived as letting him off the hook. But Barb's inner guidance was clear: her anger was hurting her much more than it hurt him. When she set her intentions, it opened up space for creative problem solving. He was still "hit and miss" with the timing, but her blood pressure was no longer rising to dangerous levels over it. In fact, she was proud of herself for coming up with solutions that met her needs instead of continuing to marinate in aggravation, frustration and rage.

SHIFTY ACTION STEP (SAS)

Here are some tools to help you deepen and integrate the shift in Chapter 3 into your life:

♥ SAS 3: Creating Powerful Divorce (or Breakup) Intentions

You are a powerful creator! The first step of the journey from where you are to where you want to be is setting your intentions. Intentions can be about what you want to do or how you want to feel or "be" inside yourself during a given situation. Intentions are definitive statements. By setting your intentions, you are pointing yourself in the direction you want to go.

There are many types of Intentions—the possibilities are endless. You can set intentions for any and every part of your life every day. You're only limited by your imagination.

Types of Intentions

How I want to be inside myself:

- Immediate: My intention for today is to notice and put my focus on all the good in my life. At the end of the day, I intend to make a list of everything that went right.

- Short Term: I intend to feel the maximum level of joy, peace and love available to me every day during this first holiday season on my own. I intend to notice and enjoy the sights, smells, tastes and special music that abound this time of year. I intend to collaborate with my kids to create some new, special traditions.

- Long Term: My intention is to get in touch with my gratitude for everything I'm learning from my divorce experience. I intend to keep a running list of my insights and "aha" moments.

What I want to do/accomplish:

- Immediate: My intention is to spend the afternoon cleaning out the garage. I intend to release items that I don't truly love or haven't used in a year's time.

- Short Term: I intend to support my radiant health and fitness by exercising at least three times this week and eating healthy food. I intend to appreciate myself for taking care of myself.

- Long Term: My intention is to speak kindly about my Ex when my kids are present. I intend to stay silent rather than expressing any negative thoughts about her/him in their presence.

An outcome I want:

- Immediate: My intention is to connect at the heart level with my kids and have fun with them as we team up to wash the car this afternoon.

- Short Term: I intend to collaborate on an agreement with my Ex about helping our son with his math this semester. I intend to put our son's needs first as we negotiate a schedule that works for both of us.

- Long Term: My intention is to set aside $20 per week into a "fun fund" that I can spend on myself any way I want to. I intend to plan fun activities for myself every month.

Now it's your turn! Your assignment is to think about what you want and create some intention statements for yourself. They can be about your divorce recovery or any other part of your life. Here are some questions to get you started:

- What do I intend for myself today?

- What do I intend for myself this week or month?

- What do I intend for myself this year?

- How do I want to feel?

- What do I want to do?

- What results do I want?

If the thought of stepping fully into your own power makes you feel squeamish, don't worry! You'll be using your powers for good…your own good, that is. Intentions are not about bending others to your will. They help you make meaningful change. One of the most destructive post-divorce mindsets is feeling powerless. The truth is that once you acknowledge the authority you have over your own life, the world opens up for you.

Visit www.DebPurdy.com/resources for a PDF of the Intention Setting Worksheet.

Quick Lifts (QL)

Here are some real, proactive steps you can take to get some immediate relief as you work through your bigger shifts.

▪ *QL 3: Good News Diet*

For better or for worse, we have the option of 24/7 consumption of the news, complete with inflammatory, derogatory and/or bleak speculations and opinions. The news is curated to focus on a tiny fraction of a story: the part that's the most shocking and upsetting. At any given time, reporters are sitting around newsrooms making lists of the top ten worst things that are happening to report. You know it's true.

I have one simple question: does the "news" fill you with optimism and motivate you to take inspired action in your life? I'm guessing "no." Marinating daily in the relentless stream of negativity from the news media is likely to leave you feeling helpless, hopeless, angry, frustrated, judgmental and uneasy—not the ideal inner conditions to make positive shifts. So stop. Just turn it off.

If you're not willing to quit engaging with the news altogether, you can easily reduce indiscriminate exposure to the daily bombardment. Instead, review the headlines online and consciously choose to delve deeper into stories that are of interest to you or are relevant to your life. But, keep in mind; knowing the grisly details of a heinous crime or latest celebrity gossip will make you feel worse, not better.

Instead, seek out and put more of your focus on what's going right in the world. Subscribe to outlets for good news stories, such as www.dailygood.org, and realize that wonderful things happen every day.

Summary

Chapter 3 discussed the second shift, transforming your intentions, and invited you to start examining your thoughts and paying attention to them. It reminded you that you don't have to believe everything you think. It gave suggestions for how to question your thoughts and use them to recreate your inner and outer world. And it introduced you to, and helped you activate, your personal super powers: awareness, choice, focus and intention. It also provided some guidelines for setting meaningful intentions.

Shift Your Story: You are the hero of your own story

You have a story about your marriage and how it ended. Our personal narratives about our hardships are important. They help us make sense of challenging life events. Telling stories is also how we connect with others. How we let them in. Difficulties arise not because you have a story, even a sad or painful one. Where you can get stuck is when you become attached to your stories and make them an essential part of your identity.

It pays to be honest with yourself about why you are telling your divorce story and how invested you are in proving a point. If the moral of your tale is what a jerk or loser your Ex is for how he or she behaved, AND you find yourself repeating it often to friends, family and whoever will listen, you may be in love with your story for all the wrong reasons.

By telling the story of how you got, or continue to get, screwed by your Ex, you are trapping yourself in the victim loop. This is a completely powerless, frustrating and toxic place to be and it keeps you from moving on. But "it's what happened" you may say. And I say, it's one way of looking at what happened—there are likely many truths unexamined that could propel you forward if you're willing to look.

> **❝** *It pays to be honest with yourself about why you are telling your divorce story and how invested you are in proving a point.* **❞**

Divorced for five years, my client Jim was still very attached to his story. He spoke often about how, during his marriage, his Ex had spent all his money on new cars, designer clothes and other material things. She used most of the money from their savings to finance a showy wedding for their daughter that they couldn't really afford. Because of that, according to Jim, he went into tremendous debt.

On the surface, it's easy to find ourselves judging his Ex and to see the "poor guy" in this no-win situation. But, when he and I dug deeper, he could see that this story was disempowering and was keeping him stuck. When we looked past his story, it became clear to him that he had been unwilling to set boundaries. His pattern was to silently seethe even as he gave in to her again and again. He had been half-hearted at best about asserting his values of living within their means.

Examining his role in events gave Jim a more empowered point of view. Because he was willing to be honest with himself, he was able to set very clear intentions about how he wanted to manage his money going forward. He also got clear on what values he wanted in his next partner.

Jim stopped telling the story about his Ex and his money woes and he stopped identifying as a "helpless bystander" to the financial mess. He was able to admit that just because he wasn't the active "spender" in the equation, he was a participant in the dynamic that led to the current situation. This gave Jim all the information he needed to change his results going forward.

Is Your Story Holding You Back?

How much time in a given day do you spend thinking about or talking about some negative aspect of your Ex, your marriage or your divorce? Here's the secret: if that's your focus, you are unconsciously setting yourself up for more of the same negative experiences and feelings.

At worst, your story can keep you stuck, sometimes for years, in a toxic stew of negativity about a part of your life. At best, it can suck the joy out of your life and unconsciously influence you as you attempt to rebuild.

How do you know if your story is sabotaging you? Ask yourself these questions:

- During conversations with your friends and

family, do you often find yourself bringing up how your divorce is impacting you or the latest antics of your Ex?

- Are you talking about your divorce or your Ex to people you've just met or don't know well?
- Do you feel your divorce and, by extension, your Ex are to blame for your current situation, feelings or challenges?
- Are you more drawn to people who sympathize and/or agree with your position?
- When someone asks you about your Ex, do you use it as an opportunity to get in a jab about him or her?
- Is there clearly a "bad" character in your story and it's not you?

If you answered yes to any of these questions, your story is holding you back. This is good to know. It's an important step in shifting beyond a limited interpretation of past events that impedes your current progress. Now, carry it a step further by taking the *Attachment-to-Freedom Scale.*

At worst, your story can keep you stuck, sometimes for years, in a toxic stew of negativity about a part of your life. At best, it can suck the joy out of your life and unconsciously influence you as you attempt to rebuild.

This scale provides a tangible way to evaluate if, and to what extent, you are attached to your story. Take a look at it and rank where you think you are now. If you're not sure, keep it out for the next week and pay attention to how you feel, how much and to whom you are talking about your divorce and whether you are feeling predominantly negative, neutral or positive about things.

On the far left of the scale, at zero, is a state of being completely identified with your story. That means that there is no separation between you and your perception of what happened to you and no other way to look at it than your point of view. On the far right of the scale is complete freedom from your story. After having used it as information to heal, you know that you are not defined by your story.

Take a look at the scale and do an honest assessment of where you are now. You can use it again when you finish the book to measure your progress.

Attachment-to-Freedom Scale

0 Attached	3 Inching Forward	5 Transitioning	7 Almost There	10 Free
• What happened to me is terrible and there's no other way to look at it. • Everyone agrees that my Ex is an awful person who made me suffer. • I constantly discuss my divorce experience with my friends. • I often tell my story to people I've just met. • I feel angry, frustrated, powerless, hurt and disillusioned.	• There might be other ways to look at my story but I have a hard time imagining them. • I'm sure most people would agree that I was mistreated. • I sometimes share my story with people I don't know well. • My divorce experience is a frequent topic of my conversations. • I feel sad, hurt, afraid and bitter.	• I'm open to the possibility of other ways to view and use my divorce experience. • I'm ready to talk to people who don't see me as a victim. • I'm getting tired of talking about my divorce experience. • I rarely tell the story to people I've just met. • I feel equal parts hopeful and sad, excited for the future and scared.	• I'm intentionally finding the gifts and lessons of my divorce. • I only discuss my story with those who support me in my personal growth. • I'm more interested in talking about what I'm creating next. • I still sometimes feel sad, angry or afraid, but I often feel powerful, excited and confident.	• I am the hero of my own story in which all of my challenges are opportunities to grow. • I selectively tell people about what I learned from my divorce experience when it feels relevant to a conversation. • I feel peace, freedom and gratitude when I think about my divorce experience.

Visit www.DebPurdy.com/resources for a PDF of the Attachment-to-Freedom Scale.

Destructive Divorce Storylines

As you work your way from Attached to Free, take a look at the three most common elements of divorce storylines that can stall your momentum. If you recognize yourself in one or more of these patterns, you now have the opportunity to rewrite your story into an empowering tool for growth.

Addiction to the Victim Loop: When telling your divorce story, playing the victim is very seductive. A victim doesn't have to take any responsibility. Hey, it's not my fault when I'm a victim. Yet, this stance takes away all of your power to make self-supporting and positive change.

I call it the victim loop because it goes around and around and never moves you forward. This is juicy to work through because it's so common to use victim-like thoughts and language during, and even long after, the divorce process. How do you know if you're circling the victim loop? You may be in this trap if:

- You completely blame your Ex for any part of your past or current circumstances.
- You can't identify any ways that you may have contributed to or participated in the unwanted results.
- You believe everything that was wrong was out of your control.

Breaking free requires the willingness to look at your own role in what went down. Maybe you didn't actively do anything, but you passively allowed things that weren't OK with you.

I once had a conversation with a friend who shared example after example of how his ex-fiancé had let him down. He ranted about her habit of excusing herself and heading off to the restroom while they were dining out together. It was common for her to leave him steaming at the table for 20 to 30 minutes. When questioned, she would become defensive and offer a myriad of excuses. It usually boiled down to her being on the phone with her mom or a friend and losing track of time. She would cancel plans at the last minute and was continually letting him down in other ways. After he explained each example, I asked him what he did about it. He had various answers, which all boiled down to "I told her how I felt, gave her a pass and made her promise to stop doing it." Yet, she continued the pattern until they broke up. He was looking at each individual incident and, with an appalled and shocked attitude, wondering why she kept doing that to him.

The better and more powerful question is why did he continue to allow it? She could not have kept doing that to him without his consent and participation in the pattern. Once we talked it through, a light bulb went on for him. He realized that he had a role and was not a victim. This opened him up to thinking about how the pattern of being let down in various ways, and silently stewing while putting up with it, had come up in his previous relationships, including his previous marriage. It also led him to taking steps to heal and create something different for himself going forward.

Holding on to the Past: I often hear people's divorce stories in social situations after I tell them about my work. Recently, I sat chatting with a lovely woman at a party. Although she was happily married with twin baby boys, she told me a detailed story about her first husband. He had cheated on her and left her for his mistress, to whom he was currently married.

Six years later, she still felt absolutely appalled. She punctuated her story with the phrase, "This is not what I would have chosen." The past was still so alive for her that it was robbing her of all the gratitude and joy available to her right now. She made it clear to me that she loved her new husband and adored her sons. Even when I gently tried to steer the conversation to the present, the majority of her focus was on her past marriage. This is an extreme example of the toxicity of holding on to the past.

> *Accepting the past and enjoying the present while taking actions to shape the future is the antidote to living in regret and holding on to the past.*

If you find yourself lamenting past decisions, either yours or your Ex-spouse's, you may be holding on to the past. Continually looking back with regret and recrimination will keep you from being fully present with your life. Accepting the past and enjoying the present while taking actions to shape the future is the antidote to living in regret and holding on to the past.

Arguing with Reality: When you wish things were different than what they are, you are arguing with reality. If you're thinking or saying things like:

- I'm frustrated or angry about what he or she is saying.
- This shouldn't be so hard.
- He or she should be different/act differently.
- I should have, or shouldn't have, done this or that.
- This shouldn't be happening/things should be different.

Thoughts like these represent your resistance to what's happening and they cause you to suffer. It's been said that arguing with reality is like getting angry at the sun for coming up. Another popular analogy is comparing it to banging your head against the wall and saying, "This wall should be soft," "It shouldn't hurt to bang my head" or "Who keeps putting this wall here?"—all while continuing to bang your head.

Byron Katie, author of *Loving What Is*, is quoted as saying, "When you argue with reality you lose, but only 100 percent of the time." Everything changes, whether we like it or not. The suffering comes in when we're attached to how that change should look.

Rachel's Ex, Simone, was a highly educated woman who was perpetually underemployed. This was particularly frustrating to Rachel since she had made many sacrifices during their ten-year relationship to help put

Simone through school. They'd had an agreement. Once Simone finished her degree, she would get a great job and support Rachel in leaving her corporate job and starting her own bookkeeping business.

That never happened. Despite her newly minted MBA, Simone jumped from one entry-level job to another, barely making ends meet. When their relationship dissolved, Rachel felt bitter because Simone would never be keeping her part of their bargain. Our first few coaching sessions consisted of her rants. "I can't believe she didn't keep her promise" and "It's not right" were on a constant loop in her mind.

As long as she clung to the injustice of the situation, Rachel remained in a constant state of upset, making it difficult for her to move confidently into the next phase of her life. Her shift was gradual, from "This shouldn't be happening" to "This is what's happening" to "How can I support myself and move forward from here?"

Once she learned how to accept the reality of the situation, she was able to take proactive steps to change the part she could control. Instead of focusing on what Simone didn't do, she started planning what she herself wanted to do. Rachel realized that the same resourcefulness she had demonstrated in juggling two jobs to support Simone could be put to use in supporting herself. She made a two-year plan to transition out of her job into her own business.

Learning how to accept reality is a process. The first step is to notice every time you complain about something (this traffic is brutal) and practice finding the gifts in your situation. Ask yourself, "Is there anything in this situation that can work to my advantage?" For example, "Traffic is not my favorite, but I'll use this time to listen to my audio book."

SHIFTY ACTION STEP (SAS)

Here are some tools to help you deepen and integrate the shift in Chapter 4 into your life.

SAS 4: Gifts and Blessings Inventory

Divorce stories often focus on the disappointment, guilt or shame of divorce. You can enhance your level of healing and acceptance when you reframe your stories. Recognizing and identifying the gifts and blessings of your experience is a great way to begin to rewrite your divorce narrative. You can actively change how you feel about your current experience by changing your story about it.

Your opportunity here is to reframe the experience for yourself and elevate the way you think about, and talk about, your marriage and divorce experience. You shift the focus to what you learned and what you gained. Recognizing and identifying the gifts and blessings of your experience is a great way to begin to reframe your divorce experience for yourself and change your conversations about it.

Remember, every negative experience provides information and opportunities for you. By working with those, you're training yourself to find them and use them for your benefit. This takes gratitude and meaning to a deep level.

Here are some questions to help you get access to your inner gifts and blessings inventory. Don't worry if not much comes to you the first time you do this. Just asking these questions will help the answers occur to you over time. Keep a running list that you add to as insights come to you:

What am I grateful for? Although divorce is a loss, it's also an opportunity to refocus and appreciate what you have. Part of what you can gain from divorce is a deeper recognition and appreciation of the good in your life. List everything you can think of for which you are grateful right now. If you have enough food to eat, a warm place to sleep and shelter from the elements, start there.

How has my divorce opened my heart? Emotional pain can open your heart and allow you to move deeper into compassion for yourself and others. Check in and see if this is true for you. If so, it's a gift you can include on your list.

What do I know about myself now that I didn't know before and how will I use this knowledge to make my life better? Marriage and divorce are rich sources of information about yourself and what's really important to you. By putting your focus on your role in your marriage dynamic and how you participated in the relationship, you can decide how well it worked for you. If it didn't turn out as expected, you can work to consciously heal and release your old patterns to create something different and better for yourself going forward. Document these insights as they come up—they are the "lottery winnings" of divorce.

What am I choosing for myself next? Like many of us, you may have chosen your ex-spouse based solely on chemistry—physical attraction and the excitement that's present in the initial stages of romance when everything feels amazing. Now, you know from experience that those things alone are not enough to create a wonderful and lasting relationship (this knowledge is a gift in itself). Use the knowledge you've gained during your marriage and think about what qualities are really important to you for the long haul. Start a running list of your relationship requirements for next time. These insights are a gift—add them to your list.

What relationships do I have now that I wouldn't have had if I hadn't partnered with my Ex? Your children, if you had them together, belong on your list as well as stepchildren. But also think about friends and family that you've gained as a result of your marriage. If you are close with your Ex's family and value those relationships, they count as gifts.

You can even include relationships and experiences you've gained since your divorce. For example, maybe you joined a hiking group after your divorce that you never would have joined if you were still married. The experiences and relationships you now enjoy would count as gifts of your divorce. Think about any relationships that may have deepened because of your divorce—also gifts!

What am I free to do now that I didn't allow myself to do before? Sometimes, it takes a huge life change to shift you out of your comfortable groove and make you try something new. Are you pursuing something you've always wanted to do but have never done? Or are you finally ready to find a career that feeds your passion for life? Are you using this new beginning to start on the path to self-discovery? These are gifts.

Don't be limited by this list. You may think of more types of gifts than I've listed here. Once you set your intention to focus on and find the gifts and blessings of your marriage and divorce, they will start becoming more obvious to you!

♥ SAS 5: Active Self-Compassion

It's very common for divorce to bring up feelings of guilt and shame, regardless of whose decision it was to end the marriage. Being kind and compassionate with yourself is a powerful step toward healing. It is an antidote to the pain of self-judgment and self-criticism. Self-compassion is allowing yourself to focus your loving on yourself. It's true that sometimes, you don't measure up to your own aspirations. Self-compassion is the act of giving yourself space for falling short, getting up and carrying on. It's also giving yourself grace and recognizing that, like everyone else, you're an imperfect human doing the best you can.

This is a step you might be tempted to skip. Don't.

Holding yourself in contempt as a form of self-punishment is a pattern that doesn't serve you. The reality is that ongoing and unaddressed guilt and shame are toxic emotional waste. When these feelings come up or recur, recognize them for what they are—an opportunity. They are coming up to be acknowledged and released, not pushed back down only to come back up on endless repeat. When you address and release them, you free yourself from your self-imposed bondage. If you feel like you "deserve" to feel guilty because of your past, you are completely missing the point. You deserve your own love and forgiveness. It may be counter intuitive, but self-forgiveness is a selfless act. It's the most direct route to growing into a more loving, forgiving and compassionate person.

> **❝** *You deserve your own love and forgiveness. It may be counter intuitive, but self-forgiveness is a selfless act. It's the most direct route to growing into a more loving, forgiving and compassionate person.* **❞**

How to "Show Up" for Yourself with Compassion

Find a quiet place where you won't be disturbed. Grab some tissues and possibly a pen and notebook in case you want to capture any insights that result from this process. Think about the situation that is causing you to experience pain, guilt or shame (the ending of your marriage, for example). Allow yourself to fully experience the feelings that come up. Identify the judgments you've placed against yourself regarding this situation, such

- I should have worked harder to keep my ~~marriage~~ together.
- I failed as a wife/husband.
- I've made bad decisions that hurt other people.

Remind yourself that the essence of who you really are is not your feelings, thoughts or behaviors. Your feelings, thoughts and past behaviors are simply information you can use to learn and grow. You are lovable and inherently worthy of love, no matter what.

In your mind's eye, think of a person, animal or place that inspires feelings of love and affection. This could be a child or another person you love, a beloved pet, a beautiful sunset or even a treasured memory. Feel the love that rises up inside of you when you think of this person, animal, place or memory. Notice the loving energy of the feeling and imagine it as a glowing white light that emanates from your heart and surrounds and fills your whole body.

Now, from this place, share the loving with yourself by placing your hand on your heart. Replace each judgment statement with a compassionate, self-forgiving one. Say it out loud to yourself. For example:

- I forgive myself for judging myself as not working hard enough to hold my marriage together. The truth is that I'm human and I did the best I could at that time. I'm ready to learn from my past and use the information to shape a better future.

- I forgive myself for judging myself as a failure as a wife/husband. The truth is, it took courage to get married in the first place. Because I did that, I've learned how to have more compassion for myself and others.
- I forgive myself for my past decisions and actions. I will use what I'm learning to do better. The truth is that all of my power is in the present and what I choose to do next.

Say as many "forgiveness" and "truth" statements as come forward to you. Close the process when you feel a shift into a more loving, compassionate and positive frame of mind. Acknowledge yourself for your willingness to work with yourself and free yourself of self-judgment.

Guilt and regret will separate you from joy in the present—don't do that to yourself. Take whatever steps necessary to give yourself grace. Let it be OK to have made decisions in the past that you wouldn't make today knowing what you know now. The sooner you can forgive yourself and accept that you did the best you could, the more joy you will be capable of now and going forward.

Do You Need to Make Amends?

As part of this process, you may become aware that your behaviors or actions may have harmed another person in some way—either intentionally or unintentionally. You can clean up this outstanding issue by owning up to it and apologizing without making excuses. It's important to let go of any expectations about the other person's reaction or acceptance of your apology. Whether or not they can let it go has no bearing on whether or not you let it go. Make a heart-felt apology and, if necessary, make amends. Do your self-forgiveness process, set your intention to do no harm moving forward and let it go.

Quick Lifts (QL)

Here is a real, proactive step you can take to get some immediate relief as you work through your bigger shifts.

■ QL 4: Create an "Advisory Board" of Personal Heroes

Actively identify people, living or dead, whose lives inspire and uplift you. Maybe it's someone who overcame extreme trauma at the hands of others and not only survived, but was able to forgive. Or, it could be someone who beat seemingly insurmountable odds to do something extraordinary. Or, it could be someone who approached life with wisdom, creativity and grace.

Print out photos and/or quotes and put them up where you can see them. Think of them as your personal advisory board. Imagine that they are guiding you and cheering you on. Abraham Lincoln and Steve Jobs are two of mine. I ask myself, "What would Abraham Lincoln say right now?" or "How would Steve Jobs creatively approach this challenge?" Or, I read a quote from Eleanor Roosevelt and imagine that I possess her courage and strength of heart and, suddenly, I do.

Need a Helping Hand

Sometimes, it can be difficult to identify your relationship stories and patterns on your own. Or, for some, directing love, forgiveness and compassion toward themselves is too difficult. If you're struggling with this, or your feelings are overwhelming, consider working with a coach or therapist. Getting the extra help you need to get you through the rough spots is smart and self-supporting!

Summary

Chapter 4 discussed the third shift, transforming your story. It talked about the importance of personal narrative while describing the perils of "falling in love" with your story. It described the three most common destructive story lines and gave you a way to measure your progress toward freeing yourself from over-identifying with your story.

CHAPTER 5

Shift on Your Ex: Can't we all just get along?

We've all heard of a fairytale marriage. How about a fairy-tale divorce? Most people consider the possibility of genuinely friendly ex-spouses in the same realm as unicorns and Bigfoot. Some have claimed to witness these mythical creatures but few have verifiable proof.

Our culture has normalized nastiness as the default for divorcing couples. The media promotes conflict and bad behavior as entertainment. The internet mob mentality ranges from suspicion to open hostility toward those who proclaim goodwill in the face of divorce. Celebrity couples are viciously mocked for attempting "conscious" divorces that promote collaboration over animosity.

It's no wonder that, up to this point, we've accepted

this as "the way it is." It's time to rethink the culture of divorce. We've been taught to end our marriages in ways that often guarantee painful results for all involved. What if there was another way?

I remember reading about a newly divorced couple that stood outside the courthouse immediately after their divorce was finalized by the judge and took a post-divorce selfie together. When questioned about this, the pair responded with a very healing and self-supportive point of view. They decided to choose for themselves what their divorce would mean. Both partners said they were glad the marriage had happened. Even in the face of a divorce, they chose for it to mean they were blessed enough to have had the experience of being married to one another. They viewed their divorce as the beginning of their friendship. They chose love in the face of a challenge.

> **❝** *It's within your power to reinvent what divorce means to you. Often, this will have a ripple effect on your Ex. But, even if it doesn't, you can still achieve peace and equanimity within yourself.* **❞**

This couple provides a great example of choosing peace, love and grace no matter what you're going through. You can choose what the experience of divorce will mean to you, your family and your friends. This couple said they posted the picture because they didn't want the people close to them to feel like they had to choose sides or feel awkward around them.

If your relationship with your Ex is not anywhere

near selfie status, or you're willing but you think your ex-spouse would sooner eat a bug than take a selfie with you, not to worry. It's within your power to reinvent what divorce means to you. Often, this will have a ripple effect on your Ex. But, even if it doesn't, you can still achieve peace and equanimity within yourself.

Decide What You Want

If you allow yourself, you can choose to view your marriage as an intense laboratory experiment which provided you with the opportunity to work out your unresolved issues—your core programs and beliefs—with someone who was reflecting them back to you. We all know someone who marries a person with traits similar to one of his or her parents, then divorces that person only to marry someone else with the same characteristics. The woman who grew up with a hyper-critical parent marries a demanding partner who is perpetually dissatisfied with her. The man with the cold and distant parent marries a partner who is incapable of true intimacy. Our goal

> *If you're open to it, the next leap is getting in touch with your gratitude for your ex-spouse for his or her role in your evolution.*

should be to proactively learn the lessons and heal the patterns so we can get off the hamster wheel of dysfunction.

If you are with me so far, you are considering the idea of using your marriage and divorce as an intense course in Me School. From this perspective, your Ex is and was your lab partner in your life experiment. You now have the opportunity to actively and specifically shift the way you hold your Ex inside yourself. Only when you do that will you have a chance to change the external dynamic.

If you didn't have children together, you have the option to create some other kind of relationship, say, friendship or even extended family. Hey, you loved each other enough to marry in the first place, so you don't have to give up being family just because the marriage didn't pan out. For example, one of my clients chose to be on the emotional support team for his ex-wife as she navigated her way through breast cancer.

You could also distance yourself completely, if that works best for you—or anything in-between. Most important is how you feel inside about your divorce. Even if you choose to cut ties, your goal is to appreciate the opportunities for growth and inner peace when it comes to thinking about your ex-partner and your past relationship. If you're open to it, the next leap is getting in touch with your gratitude for your ex-spouse for his or her role in your evolution.

Having kids together makes the stakes higher. In that case, your invitation is to transition from spouses to co-parenting partners. You can still be an extended family if you choose it—with everyone's partners and kids included. My Ex still comes over on Christmas morning to be there when our kids wake up. Or, you can simply be civil when you exchange kids. Again, the invitation is to drop the blame game and truly operate from acceptance inside yourself.

But, What If My Ex Is a #$@&%*!?

Ah, the million dollar question! This all works unless your Ex is a cheating bastard or a psycho bitch, right? Well, no. It works no matter what your Ex did in the past or how he or she behaves now. That's because this isn't about your Ex; it's about you. You may be thinking, "Yeah, right!" But, hear me out.

The good news is that you can do this on your own. In other words, your success isn't dependent on your ex-spouse jumping on the bandwagon with you or on him or her changing their wayward ways and begging your forgiveness for past transgressions. Your primary objective is inner peace, regardless of what your Ex says or does or doesn't do. This includes what he or she did or didn't do in the past.

If your Ex "done you wrong" in some way, and you're not willing to look at your role in the relationship dynamic, you may be holding on to your victim story, which, as we discussed in Chapter 4, will stop your progress dead in its tracks. Or, you could be holding on to

If your Ex continues to show up as a jerk as we speak, no sweat. Think of him or her as one of your key professors in Life School who is offering you a master's level course. The subject of the course depends on what you most need to learn.

the past or resisting reality. Wouldn't it be wonderful to remember your past the way an anthropologist examines artifacts? Viewing it as an interesting time in history, and using the experience to learn more about what it means to be human, is what you're on your way to right now.

If your Ex continues to show up as a jerk as we speak, no sweat. Think of him or her as one of your key professors in Life School who is offering you a master's level course. The subject of the course depends on what you most need to learn. I needed to learn to stand up for myself, face my fear of anger and let go, once and for all, of people pleasing. That didn't happen overnight, but embracing each encounter as a chance to practice new skills bolstered my confidence and changed my life on many levels.

My client Spencer sincerely wanted to figure out how to make this shift. He considered his Ex, with whom he has a toddler, absolutely toxic, irrational and manipulative. Carl seemed to love to push Spencer's buttons. They had different parenting styles and Carl would send nastily worded e-mails haranguing Spencer about how he was ruining their daughter. Carl spread his decidedly negative opinions about Spencer and his life choices to anyone who would listen, reveling in the victim mode and actively blaming Spencer for everything that he thought was wrong with his life. He was not shy about laying on the guilt. When he got demoted at his job, he blamed Spencer, saying the stress of the divorce distracted him from his work. Since Spencer had made the decision to leave the marriage, a part of him felt like he deserved some of the anger Carl was directing toward him.

For his part, Spencer was always on the defensive. He answered every one of Carl's angry e-mails with a fierce rebuttal. He did damage control, where he could, with friends and family. He tried to make sure everyone knew his side of the story. This led to giving examples of Carl's craziness and doing some trash talking of his own. He grew exhausted, angry and stressed by the constant barrage of negativity, blame and the never-ending job of defending himself.

Spencer realized that, for the good of his daughter and his own peace of mind, something had to change. He also realized he could only control his own actions and attitude. He started to think of his Ex as "Professor Carl," who was doing him a service by unknowingly assisting with his personal growth. Every time Carl did something that upset him, Spencer said to himself, "school is in session."

This huge shift in attitude supported Spencer's change in response. During our coaching calls, he identified his strategies to deal with Carl's most common attacks. Instead of being reactive, Spencer took a minute to thoughtfully decide how he wanted to respond. He stopped sending his counter arguments to Carl's e-mail attacks. Really, what was the point? He was never going to change Carl's mind. Instead, he only addressed the part of the messages that had logistical details about their daughter. He confirmed a pick-up time in one courteous sentence, ignoring the rest of the vitriol. To his surprise, when he stopped engaging, the e-mail rants began to taper off.

He stopped trying to defend himself with their mutual friends. He realized that those who really care about him already know he's a good dad doing the best he can in a difficult situation. As for the rest of the peanut gallery, they were enjoying the drama. He began to release them from his life.

He worked on forgiving himself for ending his marriage and really embraced the new paradigm of marriage as a learning lab. Releasing his guilt let him see that Carl was directing his anger and fear toward Spencer instead of dealing with his own issues. When Spencer stopped taking the attacks personally, he was able to truly move into compassion as he watched Carl struggle. He even began to wish Carl well. Ultimately, Spencer hoped Carl would get to the level of peace that he, Spencer, was actively cultivating.

Because he really worked to understand and began to own his role in their relationship pattern, Spencer managed to change the pattern. As is frequently the case, as he began to change toward his Ex, Carl began to respond. If you asked Carl, he would still give you a litany of reasons why the divorce and its aftermath were all Spencer's fault. However, he's slowly gotten easier for Spencer to work with and the drama level has nosedived. Best of all for Spencer, he knows that he'll be able to maintain his equilibrium, regardless of what Carl says or does. And he finds that very liberating.

Create Your Vision

You may be starting to have an idea about the kind of new relationship you intend with your Ex. From here, it's time to get more specific with your vision. The first step is to think about what an ideal relationship with your Ex-spouse would look like. Use that as the basis for your vision. Really go for the best case scenario, regardless of how nasty or unpleasant things may be right now. Even if you can't believe it will ever be anything approaching civil, if your best case would be relaxed and friendly, that's what you should shoot for. Start by considering the questions in this short quiz to get your wheels turning.

Choose as many answers as apply for each question and/or write in your own.

1. **What kind of relationship would work best for your life?**
   a. I will always consider my Ex to be part of my extended family.
   b. I want to keep a post-divorce friendship with my Ex.
   c. I intend to maintain a collaborative co-parenting partnership with my Ex.
   d. Being civil with my Ex is enough for me.
   e. I will rarely or never be in contact with my Ex.
   f. Other: _____

2. **How do I want feel inside myself when it comes to my Ex?**
   a. Completely Neutral.
   b. Peaceful and Relaxed.
   c. Friendly Equanimity.
   d. Grateful and Open-Hearted.
   e. Other: _____

3. **What's at stake?**
   a. My kids are still minors and a good working relationship between my Ex and me is extremely important to the well-being of everyone involved.
   b. My kids are grown and out of the house and a good relationship will be emotionally healthy for me and make things easier and more pleasant for everyone involved.
   c. Kids are not an issue but feeling goodwill toward my Ex will be emotionally healthy for me.
   d. Kids are not an issue but feeling neutral toward my Ex is a big step up and will be emotionally healthy for me.
   e. Other: _____

Review your answers. Use them to get clear on what's important to you. Once you're clear on what you want, you can more easily and effectively move toward it. An Ideal Scene is a great tool for getting your vision down on paper so you can see it. The purpose is to connect you with your goal. Here's an example of the Ideal Scene that I did right in the middle of the worst and ugliest part of my divorce.

Deb's Ideal Scene: Relationship with Ex

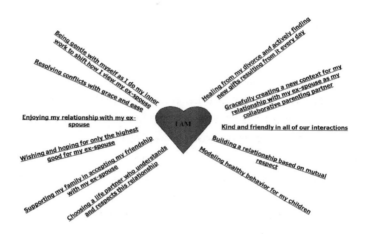

At the time that I wrote this, I realized that no one had a bigger stake in my relationship with my Ex than my kids and me. My attorney had only one agenda, and that was decidedly short term. My family was determined to see me as the innocent victim and wouldn't even hear me when I talked about my contribution to the dysfunction of my marriage. I realized that this change had to come from inside of me, from my own intuition about what I wanted to create for my kids and myself.

When you read my Ideal Scene, you'll notice that it doesn't have anything for him to do. It's all about what's going on inside of me. When I wrote this, I did not know how I was going to get there. In fact, I only partially believed it was possible, but it has all come to fruition and more—everything turned out even better than what I wrote.

It's Your Turn

Create your own Ideal Scene for your relationship with your Ex. Don't stop at incrementally better than it is now, but really go for what it would be if it was truly a blessing in your life a year from now. What you're doing is thoughtfully deciding what you want that relationship to be (or at least how you want to think about him or her inside yourself).

Declaring the outcome you intend is an important first step in creating your life the way you want it.

Writing Guidelines:

Your Ideal Scene should be specific and use energizing, positive language that inspires you. It should also be written in the present tense, as if it were happening right now. Make it 50 percent believable and don't include outcomes that depend on others to come to fruition. Here are a few examples:

Not Believable: I am pleased that my Ex has completely stopped lashing out at me.

50% Believable: I am peaceful inside myself when

my Ex lashes out because I know that it's not r‹
me and I non-judgmentally and compassionate.., ...
that, right now, he's unaware of his own unresolved issues.

Not Believable: I am happy that my Ex realized her big mistake in leaving me.

50% Believable: I accept my Ex's decision to leave our marriage and I've found the strength of heart to uncover the gifts and blessings of the past and take them into my future.

Not Believable: I am enjoying more attention from my friends who are working hard to cheer me up.

50% Believable: I am loving the results of my strong intention to care for myself while I recover from my divorce and am finding great joy in making time every week to do things I love to do.

You can use the blank template provided here or simply draw a heart in the center of a blank sheet and write the words "I AM" in the middle of it. Write in lines starting from the center and radiating out. Name your Ideal Scene at the top (e.g. Ideal Scene: Peaceful Co-Existence with Ex) and write "This or something better for the highest good of all concerned" at the bottom. This phrase keeps you open to having wonderful things come forward in your life that you can't even imagine right now.

Make sure you have some quiet time to focus and reflect when you sit down to create your Ideal Scene. Light a candle or play some relaxing music if that helps you to shift from your day-to-day mindset to get in touch with your heart-felt intention for this aspect of your life. When you've finished, put it someplace you can see it or easily find it and refer to it. You don't have to show it to anyone. If you decide to share it, make sure to do so with a trusted person who will support your intentions. This is your blueprint for change.

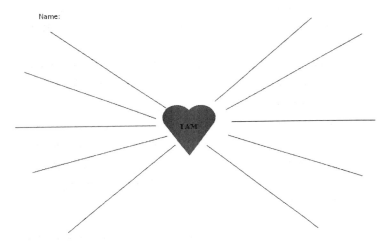

Name:

I AM

Visit www.DebPurdy.com/resources for a PDF of an Ideal Scene Template.

An Invitation to Accelerate Your Results

Ideal Scenes are very powerful. If you really want to progress even faster, here's an invitation to really go for it. I call it inner work that has an outer impact:

- No matter what stress or hassle your Ex is wreaking in your life, spend a few minutes each day imagining him or her surrounded in an aura of calm, good humor and acceptance.

- Find a picture of your Ex that you like, maybe from when you first met, and send it love and goodwill every day. Say to the photo: "Hey, we both did the best we could with what we knew. I don't like everything you did, everything you said or every decision you made. I know you probably feel the same about me. But, I'm willing to give you grace and I'm willing to give myself grace. I'm willing to embrace the gifts and lessons. I'm ready to move on."

- If you have kids, look at them and know that without your Ex, you would not have them. You can't regret your Ex without regretting your kids. Bask in gratitude for your past choices that brought your children into your life.

Think of the love you are sending to your Ex as a radiant light that illuminates, enfolds and uplifts you and him or her. It's not romantic love, but rather like the love of a beautiful sunset—an expansive, open heartedness in the presence of the struggles of a fellow human being.

Divorce Vows

You can do all of the above in this chapter (and this book for that matter) without the knowledge or consent of your Ex. As I've said, it's not about your Ex, it's about you and managing how you feel inside yourself. You don't need to share any of this process with your Ex for it to work beautifully for you. However, if you get to the point where you think your Ex may be open to it, this process includes an optional cooperative aspect, if and when you feel ready.

One morning right after I had created my Ideal Scene, but before anything had changed in the tone of our post-divorce relationship, I met my Ex for breakfast to discuss some outstanding issues. It was a very emotional meeting. I had made this shift but it was still very new and he still felt deeply upset about what was happening. We painfully went over the things we had to discuss. As we were walking out of the restaurant, both in the grip of our own anguish and grief, I asked him to wait a moment. He turned and looked at me. Standing next to our cars in the parking lot I said, "I have a vision of us at our daughter's college graduation. We are sitting in the same row with our extended family and we are laughing and crying because we are so proud of how we worked together so beautifully to raise our daughters all these years. We are grateful to each other for our collaboration and we feel very affectionate toward each other. I am going to do everything in my power to bring this vision into reality." He did not say a word. He got into his car and drove away.

I held on to my vision. I know in my heart that day marked the beginning of a shift in him. I later reinforced it by reminding him over the following weeks and months that we are still partners, only in a different context. I continued to share my vision of us working together cooperatively for the highest good of our daughters.

Important note! I said all of these things to him without any expectations. I didn't want anything from him. I was putting it out there for me. I was anchoring and solidifying my intention for myself. I even shared my vision of our future partners all being part of a wonderful extended family. Guess what? That's exactly what happened.

If you get strong in your intention, and you feel that you can handle it if your still-angry Ex mocks or rejects your vision, you may want to consider sharing it with him or her. You may not be comfortable or feel it is right to share—that's completely fine. Or, you may want to wait until he or she has some time to adjust. Follow your intuition.

If you do decide to share, and your vision is well received, you can consider creating a simple Divorce Vow to solidify your new normal. It can be as simple as this:

As cooperative co-parents, we vow to discuss any issues and disagreements with kindness, patience and mutual respect. If one or both of us gets upset, we'll take a break and come back when we're both calm. We vow to always speak kindly about each other to our kids.

You can add to it or change it depending on your situation. This type of agreement will make all the difference to your kids. They will gain tremendous peace and security knowing that their parents have agreed to work together at this level.

SHIFTY ACTION STEP (SAS)

Here are some tools to help you deepen and integrate the Chapter 5 shift into your life:

SAS 6: Let It OUT

Feelings of anger, hurt, fear and pain are completely normal as you go through the divorce process and even long afterwards. Milestones such as the holidays or your Ex meeting someone new can trigger these feelings all over again.

One great way to acknowledge and process these feelings is with a writing purge. This is a special technique for letting feelings come up and out and can be very cathartic any time you are feeling sad, hurt, angry, afraid or overwhelmed. Here's how you do it:

1. Set aside at least 15 minutes and up to an hour. Find a quiet place where you won't be disturbed and sit down with a pen and some paper. Get some tissue ready just in case.

    Although you might be tempted, don't do your writing purge on a computer because it doesn't have the same impact. The act of purge writing is a kinesthetic activity and it can release long suppressed thoughts and feelings. At times, you may end up writing very forcefully so a pen is better than a pencil.

2. Begin by writing down your thoughts as they come into your mind. This is stream-of-consciousness writing, so don't worry about writing in complete sentences or even making sense. Just jot down whatever is coming up and let it out on the paper. Don't hold back. Say what you want to say. Curse, swear and record whatever is coming up inside of you. Continue writing until you feel emptied out. You may yell or cry as you're writing and emotions come to the surface—whatever, it's OK.

   In some instances, you will find yourself writing as fast as you can, and at other times, you will be writing slowly. Throughout this process, you should be writing continuously, because there are always thoughts in your mind—write them down, even if they are "I don't know why I'm doing this" or " What should I write next?"

3. This is very important—when you feel complete, DO NOT read back through what you wrote or you will take the energy and emotions back in again. Also, immediately remove the pages from your home. You can either tear them into tiny pieces and put them in an outside trash bin or safely burn them (I crunch my pages into balls and burn them in an empty terra cotta flower pot in the backyard. I watch it burn and when only ashes are left, I make sure to put some water in the pot to be safe).

Some people still feel the energy of what they have released even after they have torn up or burned the pages. It's important to stop the process when you stop the writing. When you're complete with the writing, get up right away and move around. Stretch, drink some water and move on to something else after you've destroyed your pages. Do NOT think back over what you wrote—Let it go.

4. Don't talk about what you wrote with friends or others.

5. Seek the assistance of a coach or therapist if you need support processing your feelings.

You can do this every day or once in a while when you feel you want to release pent up feelings. Whatever works best for you!

♥ SAS 7: Is It Time to Use the "F" Word?

Wounds from your marriage and divorce can leave you with lingering bitterness, anger and hostility. These emotions don't hurt your Ex, but science says they have a real and lasting negative effect on you. You may have heard the oft quoted saying that "holding on to anger is like drinking poison and expecting the other person to die." It's a very apt metaphor for the impact of holding on to your anger and, in many ways, letting it inform your thoughts, words and actions.

Forgiving your Ex is for your own benefi
ting him or her off the hook. In fact, it has vei
with the other person. The act of forgiveness actually lets
you off the hook of self-imposed suffering.

What exactly is forgiveness?

Forgiveness is a conscious decision to let go. When you
truly decide you are going to forgive your Ex for his or
her past and current actions, you are halfway there. Ex-
perts who teach forgiveness make it clear that forgiveness
does not mean condoning the actions of the other person.
While forgiveness can help repair a damaged relationship,
it doesn't obligate you to reconcile with the other person
or release them from any le-
gal accountability. Instead,
forgiveness will bring you
peace of mind and free you
from the toxic stew of anger
and resentment. While you
recognize the pain you suf-
fered, that pain does not de-
fine you. You may never feel
positive feelings toward your
Ex, but you may be able to
come to a place of acceptance. That means that thinking
over the past no longer triggers your wrath. In fact, forgiveness opens you up to getting in touch with the good
that came out of your situation.

> **❝**Forgiveness will bring you peace of mind and free you from the toxic stew of anger and resentment. While you recognize the pain you suffered, that pain does not define you.**❞**

It's important to realize that this is a process. It may happen in a flash of enlightenment, but, more than likely, it will take time. Be gentle with yourself. If you're not ready, that's okay, too.

A Path to Forgiveness

There's no one right way to go about the forgiveness process. Books and websites offer many wonderful forgiveness methods. Find one that feels good to you. I've outlined my path to finding forgiveness below:

First, decide that you are going to start the process. This is a conscious decision. Only you know if you're ready and willing to forgive. You can reinforce your decision to forgive by writing down your intention.

Second, acknowledge your pain. Let yourself feel your sadness, anger and grief for what happened and what didn't happen. You may be dealing with a major betrayal, or it may have been a thousand garden-variety relationship disappointments over the years that led to animosity and resentment. Either way, you are letting go of what you wanted your relationship to be. Only after you acknowledge your feelings and give them their due can you begin to move into forgiveness. Recognizing your pain ultimately supports your capacity to begin to accept and move on.

Third, stop taking it personally. This is a tough one because you experience the impact of the other person's words and actions as up close and personal. Here's the deal: All external behaviors are mirrors of the internal landscape. If another person is acting hurtful, that's coming directly from his or her unhealed wounds about which they are very likely unaware. The deeper a person is wounded and lacking in self-awareness about it, the more damage they may cause to others—mental, emotional and physical.

Orient yourself to the fact that another person's words and actions, although they may impact your experience, aren't really about you. Instead, they are a reflection of that person's inner, wounded self, lashing out from fear and pain. Don't make your Ex's unkind words, lying, cheating or other misdeeds mean anything about you, because they do not.

The more you can move from opponent to scientific observer of your Ex, the easier it will be to stop taking things personally. This is a huge step toward letting go. Don't forget that you, too, have an unconscious wounded self. Look at your own thoughts and behaviors for clues to your own unhealed wounds and put your focus on increasing your own self-awareness and healing yourself.

Fourth, rewrite your story. Use the gifts and blessing inventory from Chapter 4 to rewrite your marriage and divorce story with an emphasis on what you learned and gained from the experience. Think of other ways you can look at and interpret your story that are more empowering. That includes taking responsibility for your role in your relationship dynamic.

Fifth, take inspiration and encouragement from others who've forgiven the unforgivable. Many people in this world have forgiven unimaginable cruelty and heinous acts of violence. These individuals give us the model for what that looks like. They also give us permission to forgive. It helped me to read stories of what I call "heroic" forgiveness as inspiration on my own forgiveness journey. Here are a few wonderful resources I found that supported me in my own process:

www.learningtoforgive.com
www.theforgivenessproject.com
www.forgivenessday.org

Quick Lifts

Here's a proactive step you can take to get some immediate relief as you work through your bigger shifts.

▓ *QL 5: Joy to the World!*

Start a running Joy List, a list of activities that bring you joy, make you laugh, relax you or are simply fun. Start keeping a running list of activities that sound fun and pleasurable to you. It could be anything from taking a bubble bath or watching a funny movie to scheduling lunch with friends or taking horseback riding lessons. Then, choose something on the list and do it.

Here are a few questions to ask yourself as you make your Joy List:

- What have I always wanted to do but have never done?

- What do I love to do but don't take time for?

- What makes me feel totally pampered and decadent?

- What inspires me and brings me inner peace?

- What makes me laugh?

- What makes my body feel good?

- What topics/subjects capture my attention and spark my imagination?

- What did I love to do when I was 5, 10, 12, 16, 25?

- Who do I enjoy being with?

- Where have I always wanted to go?

- What's on my bucket list?

My Joy List

Start your list by brainstorming ten things you want to try or do more of:

1. _____

2. _____

3. _____

4. _____

5. _____

6. _____

7. _____

8. _____

9. _____

10. _____

Choose one thing from your list each week, put it on your calendar and do it!

Summary

Chapter 5 discussed the fourth shift, transforming your relationship to your Ex. It invited you to make a conscious decision about how you want to think about your Ex and what you want your post-divorce relationship to look like. The chapter provided you a new tool, Ideal Scenes, to capture your vision and emphasized that any shifts you make are for you and do not require the participation of your Ex.

CHAPTER 6

Shift the Conversation: Teach people how to support you

Let's face it; most people have no idea what to say to you about your divorce, much less how to support your healing. You'll notice that the majority of people default to the socially safe route. That is to say, your Ex is fair game in the judging and bashing fest. The divorce itself is a "shame" and they are "sorry" for you. You may have even cultivated this. While this can be momentarily satisfying, it sets up unnecessary obstacles on your road to acceptance, healing and peace.

Being seen as a victim or an object of pity by your support group gives you some social rewards. You get to feel righteous. You get emotional defenders. You may even feel taken care of. Often, this is the very feeling you are missing the most as a newly single person. Unfortunately, it's not sustainable.

While well-meaning, your friends are not doing you any favors. Their sympathy does not support or help you. Think about it. When someone feels pity for you, what they're really thinking is how awful they would feel if it was happening to them. They're not bad and, of course, they're just trying to help. However, this "poor you" victim energy coming toward you does not move you forward. In fact, it

> ❝ *Being seen as a powerful person with all the inner resources you need to learn what you can, and create what you want going forward, is the best support you could ask for.* ❞

can make it harder to get unstuck and move on. Active empathy from your supporters would be much more useful to you. That is, simply being present with you without rendering an opinion or judgment and acknowledging what a wrenching experience your divorce is without feeling sorry for you. Standing by you, with the chocolate, and listening to your insights as you process this intense learning experience. Seeing you as a powerful person with all the inner resources you need to learn what you can, and create what you want going forward, is the best support you could ask for.

Do you see the difference? In the first scenario, everyone is invested in judging what's wrong and what's not working. Being seen as an object of pity creates an insidious, helpless feeling energy around you, which is stagnant and toxic. In the second scenario, the investment is in acceptance. It reflects an underlying optimism that everything that has happened is a learning opportunity that will benefit you in the long run. You are seen and supported as capable, courageous and whole as you navigate into your new life.

Maybe some friends and loved ones don't focus the judgment and disapproval exclusively on your Ex. Maybe it flows fast and furious toward you. The self-righteous among us are not shy with the divorce shaming. The attack can be open criticism or tight-lipped disapproval that sucks all the air out of the room. Either way, it's not helpful to you. I'm sure, like me, you've experienced both. Because you may agree with the judgments on some level, and they often come from those closest to you, you may find it challenging at first to effectively reframe the conversation.

While you can't control any part of what others say, think or do, you can learn to set boundaries and stick to them. You can choose to minimize your time with the pity party crowd and the Judging Judys. You can cultivate and expand relationships with those who are capable of supporting your authentic healing and you can actively teach others how to treat you through your words and actions.

Changing the Conversation with Yourself

"What was I thinking?" "Divorce is wrong!" "I'm such a mess." "How could I make such a stupid mistake?" If anyone else spoke to us the way we sometimes speak to ourselves, we would avoid them like the plague. Demeaning, disparaging or negative self-talk cranks up your stress and holds you back. The goal is to speak compassionately to yourself—just as you would to a friend.

In Chapter 3, I talked about paying attention to your thoughts. This section discusses one particular voice in your head, one I call the inner critic. You know the one. It's the voice that's always on hand to scold, point out shortcomings and trot out regrets for an in-depth review. That voice we think of as *me* is actually a collection of habitual thought patterns and unconscious programming accumulated over the years. It regurgitates the voices that influenced us growing up, including parents, teachers, sports coaches, peers, the media and our culture in general.

> *That voice we think of as me is actually a collection of habitual thought patterns and unconscious programming accumulated over the years.*

The good news is that the inner critic is NOT you. You are actually the observer of that voice and have the power to redirect it toward more self-supporting thoughts. With awareness, observation and by practicing some simple techniques, you can rewire yourself for more positive inner conversation. This, in turn, will result in more peace, joy and the confidence to set boundaries with others.

The choice comes when you notice how you're relating to yourself and you choose to be more loving. The first step in taming this inner critic is to become aware of it. It doesn't take long to get good at noticing your inner critic's voice. I am not suggesting that this aspect of you is bad or needs to be wiped out. In fact, it's probably trying to protect you in some way. Yet, like any unobserved and unquestioned pattern, it can easily run amok. Instead of judging or vilifying it, we can create a compassionate relationship with the voice and take an active role in the inner dialog.

One way to do this is to give your inner critic a name and get a mental picture of what it would look like if it were a person. A past client, Josh, started calling his inner critic Frank the Tank, and the picture that popped into his mind was a pro-wrestler. When he thought about it, he realized that the inner critic's intentions were good. Frank, who had a tenacious insistence on cataloging Josh's mistakes, was in full future-pain-avoidance mode.

Frank was a creative genius at coming up with multiple possible negative scenarios. Whenever Josh noticed Frank becoming too domineering with the negativity, he would say, "I hear you Frank, thanks for the input, but I don't need to dwell on what went wrong with my marriage. What else could you be doing to help me right now? How about helping me expand my list of gifts and blessings that came out of it?" Posing this question helped Josh turn all of that powerful energy toward generating positive and helpful ideas.

By the way, this dialog can all take place in your head! The simple action of acknowledging the inner critic and understanding that this is an aspect of yourself that you can talk to, befriend and redirect can be very liberating. Doing so disrupts the flow and shows you the separation you have from your thoughts. It helps you consciously take over command and control from the autopilot.

You may have gone your whole life up to this point thinking the voice in your head was the real you. Knowing you are the observer of the voice is the first step toward the bigger shift, but also know it will take practice to integrate this shift into your everyday awareness. Be gentle with yourself as you wake up to this way of being with yourself.

Changing the Conversation with Others

It's not unusual for family members and friends to continue to direct anger and judgment toward your Ex, even as you begin to move past those feelings. By fuming at your Ex on your behalf, your supporters are casting you in the role of helpless victim. First, know that you can't control how others feel about your Ex. Certain people may never be able to let go of the bad blood—that's not your responsibility. As peaceful as I am and have been about my Ex, for many years, a few members of my family still hold him in contempt. The truth is that self-sustaining righteous anger is more about the unresolved, and largely unconscious, issues of the person with the clenched teeth. Your Ex may be a trigger and a convenient target for a rage that actually has nothing to do with him or her.

Other people are waiting for a signal from you that

they can drop the drama when it comes to your Ex. Once they understand that you are working to move past your own anger, they will more than likely be happy to let it go as well.

The first step for both types is to control what and how much you share going forward to minimize reactiveness. If you're starting to move on but are in the habit of regularly venting to friends and family, you're stirring the pot. Save your rants for a coach, therapist, neutral friend or your journal. If you stop complaining about your Ex, others around might follow your lead and drop the subject. If you want to share something frustrating about your Ex as part of your own processing, be very selective. Share only with those who are willing to listen neutrally and, when asked, provide a voice of reason and balanced perspective.

> **❝Other people are waiting for a signal from you that they can drop the drama when it comes to your Ex. Once they understand that you are working to move past your own anger, they will more than likely be happy to let it go as well. ❞**

While changing the way you talk about your Ex will be enough for many to follow your lead, for others, you will need a more direct approach. If some of those closest to you continue to bag on your Ex even after you stop, it's time to lovingly set some boundaries. Express your appreciation for all of their love and support. Let them know you have decided to focus on the good that came out of your marriage as a way to reclaim your power and move on. Tell them that the best way they can support you going forward is to stick to the old adage, "If you can't say something nice, please don't say anything at all."

My client Pam was very close to her family who had been a huge support during her divorce. While setting boundaries was very effective with the majority, it wasn't so easy with her brother, Blake. As she started to move past her anger at her Ex, Blake could not. His continual barrage of snide comments were a guilty pleasure early on but began to wear her down.

Know that as you evolve, the people closest to you may not grow at your pace. You can keep the connection that you value while changing your approach. Pam recognized this and knew she had to give herself some space. She realized that to break the cycle, she would need to expand her social circle and try some new things. She joined a book group to start with—this got her out and talking to new people who didn't know her Ex. When she did see Blake, she changed things up. They would see a movie or go bowling instead of hanging out and talking. When they did talk, she steered the conversation toward what she, and he, were the most excited about going forward.

SHIFTY ACTION STEP (SAS)

Here are some tools to help you deepen and integrate the Chapter 6 shift into your life:

💜 SAS 8: Time Traveling for 30 Seconds a Day

Changing your inner dialog to be more loving to yourself will, quite literally, change your life. Once you do this, you will feel more confident, peaceful and happy. It will also help shield you from the judgments of others. All you need to do to jump start your self-love revival is to go back in time. I call this exercise, "seeing yourself through an angel's eye view" (if the angel image doesn't work for you, think of how a grandparent looks at a grandchild). This is simple and just takes 30 seconds a day.

- Get a picture of yourself as an infant, toddler or young child. See how darling and precious you were! If you don't have one, find a picture of a child who resembles you to represent your younger self.
- Put it in a spot where you will see it each day.
- For a few seconds every day, look into the eyes of your younger self and feel the love and compassion that wells up for that baby. Think or whisper to precious little you, "I love you," "You are precious" and "I'm here for you."
- When you really feel the love for your younger self, look into your adult eyes in the mirror and see that

the beautiful baby is still in there. Say, "I love you," "You are precious" and "I'm here for you" while looking into your own eyes.

This exercise helps you develop a loving and supportive way of seeing yourself. When you have a negative or critical thought about yourself, think of how you would talk to your innocent, trusting baby self and be as loving to yourself at that moment as you would be to her or him if she or he were right in front of you now.

SAS 9: Know What You Want (and What You Don't)

Shifting your conversations with others is a form of teaching people how to treat you. This means it's up to you to allow or not allow certain treatment. It also means you have to first get clear about how you want to be treated. For some of us, this may be the first time we ever even gave this any thought.

Go to School on It

Although you can apply this to any part of your life, we're going to focus here on how people talk to you about your Ex and your divorce. A good way to start is to use a Change Matrix to look at what you want to change about your current situation, evaluate what you are doing or not doing that contributes to what you want to change and come up with strategies to change it.

Situation to Change	My Part	My Next Move
My mom always tells me she's afraid I'll never meet anyone else.	I'm actually worried about that, too, and I sometimes tell her that and about my other worries. I know that she ruminates on them and often brings them back up to me.	• Stop talking to my mom about my worries. She can't stay positive or even neutral about my life. • Write in my journal instead. • Share only with those who are willing to listen neutrally and, when asked, provide a balanced perspective.
By convenience, my neighbors have become my default friend group. Many of them are very judgmental about my decision to leave my marriage; they aren't as friendly toward me now.	I've let people who don't have my best interests at heart too deep into my life. I've shared too much and I've limited my social circle to a very small group.	• Make a concerted effort to cultivate new friends starting now. • Connect with other people currently going through divorce. • Be more selective about who I spend time with and bring into my confidence.
My dad freely asks me a lot of intrusive questions about my divorce. It's uncomfortable to decide what and how much to say and, sometimes, I end up sharing too much.	I feel obligated to try and answer the questions because I know he cares about me. I have a hard time saying no and setting boundaries.	• Decide ahead of time exactly what I'm willing to tell him, if anything. • Answer his first question by saying, "I appreciate that you are asking out of love but I really don't want to talk about it." • If he is insistent, lovingly cut the visit or conversation short and leave.
My sister is very disapproving of my divorce and often comments that it's ruining my kids. I always feel worried, guilty and stressed after our conversations.	I want to be able to confide in my sister but she can't understand what I'm going through and doesn't know how to best support me. She loves me but she will never give me the kind of support I really need and want.	• I will acknowledge to myself that my sister is not the right confidante. • I will stop talking to her about my divorce and find a good therapist to support me in working out my feelings. • For the time being, while I'm recovering, I will limit the time we spend together.

Now it's your turn:

Situation to Change	My Part	My Next Move

Visit www.DebPurdy.com/resources for a PDF of a Change Matrix Template.

Remember, this is a process, not an event. Identifying your role in a situation and coming up with ideas for changing the dynamic takes practice. It's not usually as simple as instantly changing long-standing patterns with your family by telling them to stop bashing your Ex or judging you for your decisions. When you've taught people how to treat you one way, it may take some time to change that pattern. It may be uncomfortable for a while. Keep at it.

My client Jody had a very close relationship with her mom, Carmen, a chronic worrier with a genius for imagining worst case scenarios. Jody and Carmen told each other everything and they spent hours on the phone every week. When Jody divorced her husband, she continued that pattern with Carmen at first. But, as Jody began working with a therapist, she realized that her conversations with Carmen left her feeling stressed and anxious. While Carmen loved her daughter very much, she was continuing the pattern of focusing on everything that could go wrong. With Jody's life as her favorite topic, these conversations were becoming unbearable for Jody. With the help of her therapist, Jody began setting boundaries and limiting phone time with Carmen. She was honest with Carmen about her wish to continue a loving relationship but with new ground rules. At first, Carmen was hurt and angry. It took her some time to understand but she eventually came around. Now, their close relationship has boundaries that make it more healthy, satisfying and supportive for both women.

Quick Lifts

Here's a proactive step you can take to get some immediate relief as you work through your bigger shifts.

▪ *QL 6: Seven Minutes in Heaven*

What if you could learn an easy, painless and fast technique to kick stress to the curb and flood yourself with positive feelings that last? What if it also helped you to bounce back from emotional wounds and open your heart to more self-love and appreciation? As if that weren't enough, what if it also helped clear away hostility toward your Ex and others who populate your "bad" list?

Research demonstrates that the incredible power of loving-kindness meditation can do all of that and more. Also called metta, loving-kindness meditation is the simple practice of directing well wishes toward yourself and other people, even the ones you love to hate.

A simple loving-kindness meditation can make you feel less isolated and more connected to those around you. One study showed that a single, seven-minute loving-kindness meditation made people feel more connected to and positive about both loved ones and total strangers and more accepting of themselves. There are many variations on how to do this, but here's one I like:

1. Sit in a relaxed position and take three deep breaths to center and relax yourself.

2. Then, breathe normally as you focus c
   flowing gently in and then out.

3. Shift the focus to your heart by putting your hand
   over your heart.

4. Repeat this phrase three or four times:
   a. May I be well, May I be happy, May I be peaceful, May I be loved.

5. Now, think of someone you love and repeat these
   words three or four times:
   a. May you be well, May you be happy, May you
   be peaceful, May you be loved.

6. Now, think of someone you feel neutral about and
   repeat three or four times:

   a. May you be well, May you be happy, May you
   be peaceful, May you be loved.

7. Now, think of someone you are experiencing
   conflict with—it could be your Ex or someone
   else. Direct loving-kindness toward this person by
   repeating:

   a. May you be well, May you be happy, May you
   be peaceful, May you be loved.

   Don't be harsh with yourself if this is a challenge for you. The important thing is to stick
   with it.

8. Now, visualize love, kindness, happiness and well-
   being welling up in your heart and surrounding

you, then moving out to surround the person closest to you, the neutral person and the challenging person. Repeat:

    a. May you be well, May you be happy, May you be peaceful, May you be loved.

9. Return to yourself and carry the feelings of peace, love and wellbeing with you.

Loving-kindness meditation does far more than produce momentary good feelings. Research shows that this type of meditation measurably increases positive emotions when practiced over a two-month period. Even more compelling, the research shows that it actually leaves practitioners better able to ward off depression and to become more satisfied with life (Fredrickson, Cohn, Coffey, Pek & Finkel, 2008).

Summary

Chapter 6 discussed the fifth shift, transforming your conversations with yourself and with others. It talked about how to name and then tame your inner critic and invited you to set loving boundaries with your friends and family and teach them to better support your recovery process. It gave you tools to identify what you want to change and a way devise strategies to reframe your conversations to be more supportive.

Kids Are Shifters Too!:
Help your kids thrive after divorce

Leaving my unhappy marriage in 2005 was by far the hardest thing I've ever done. The angst, fear, stress and turmoil of the experience was only equaled by the crushing guilt I felt about how it was impacting my daughters. Ages eight and five at the time, they were broken-hearted, confused, scared and angry all at once. I'll never forget the haunted look in the eyes of my five-year-old when she asked, "Do I still have a home?"

I wondered if I was scarring them for life. I had dismantled the family they knew and loved. They didn't understand or care about any of my adult reasons. What's worse, their parents were acting like angry, distrustful strangers with each other.

I remember crying when, at the third-grade parent-teacher conference, I saw a heart-wrenching essay my older daughter had written expressing intense feelings she wasn't sharing with me. My kindergarten-aged daughter, who'd been potty trained since age two, started having "accidents" at school—a classic sign of stress. Family counseling could only do so much, and guilt was my default emotional setting. Well-meaning friends and family made me feel even worse with their fretting and speculation about the long-term impact of our broken family.

Then, one day, I had an epiphany. I realized that, while the divorce was most definitely a traumatic event in their lives, it was also a real-life lesson in resilience. I decided right then and there to be present with them and their pain. I set my intention to use the experience to teach them to recognize, feel and express their feelings. And, when it was time, I included them in the process of building our new normal in a way that worked for all of us.

Let Them Talk, Let Them Cry

When someone we love is upset or sad, many of us have a difficult time just "being" with them and their pain. We desperately want to fix it somehow or make them feel better. We say, "Don't cry" or "There are people who have it a lot worse than you do." We may even try to make them laugh or distract them in other ways. However, failing to acknowledge your kids' feelings and allowing them their full expression is the worst thing you can do. It sends the message that their feelings aren't important or, even worse, that they can't trust you with those feelings.

As hard as it is for you, especially if you're already feeling guilty, the most precious gift you can give someone in pain is to listen with a closed mouth and an open heart. Don't lecture. Don't even commiserate (that makes it about you). Don't tell them they shouldn't feel that way, don't try to solve their problem and don't give advice. These are all called "Feeling Blockers" according to Ty and Linda Hatfield, parenting coaches and founders of *Parenting From The Heart*, which offers workshops on creating the family of your dreams.

> **"** As hard as it is for you, especially if you're already feeling guilty, the most precious gift you can give someone in pain is to listen with a closed mouth and an open heart. **"**

Instead, Ty and Linda say to listen and acknowledge what you're hearing. "It looks you're feeling _____," (fill in the blank with what you are observing, such as angry, hurt, annoyed, frustrated or overwhelmed). "I would imagine you're feeling sad about not seeing your dad" or even "Uhmm, hmm" are all gentle ways to encourage your kids to open up about their feelings and needs. When you make it an ongoing habit to create a safe and loving space for your kids to share their feelings by simply listening and encouraging, you build trust. You teach them that they and their feelings are important. You give them an outlet for their pain and you strengthen your connection with them in a way that will have a much larger impact on their lives than the divorce experience.

Don't Practice Poison Parenting

Breaking up is hard to do and it may be especially hard for kids if they feel torn between warring parents. While I like to put the focus on what "to do" rather than what "not to do," there are some poison practices worth avoiding.

1. Regardless of your situation with your Ex, keep you kids out of it. Period. It's unfair and causes undue emotional stress to use your kids to deliver messages or information to your Ex. Even the most seemingly benign logistics such as pick-up times or lunch money can be charged with emotional fallout.

2. Avoid oversharing with your kids and using them as your confidants. Their own anxiety and concern for you may come across as them being supportive of you and what you're going through. However, breaking these boundaries does real damage to your kids' peace of mind. They can't handle your adult issues and emotions.

3. Similarly, don't grill your children for details when they come back from being with your Ex. This puts them in the middle, an uncomfortable emotional position. Stick to light, general questions such as "Did you have fun?" and then let it go.

4. As tempting as it is, do not trash talk your Ex to your kids or within their earshot. Bad-mouthing can include name-calling, telling the "truth" as you perceive it, blaming and criticizing. Your Ex could be the biggest jerk west of the Rockies, but he's still their dad or she's still their mom. When you say negative things about their other parent, in a very real way, you are putting your kids in an impossible situation. The unintended consequences include creating long-term psychological scars for your kids and damaging your relationship with them. In fact, it's likely to make them more sympathetic to your Ex.

Adult children of divorce report the devastating impact this nasty, trash talking habit had on them as children of divorce. It poisons parent-child relationships and it's not worth it.

If you suspect, or know, that your Ex is "throwing you under the bus" when it comes to your kids, take the high road. If they bring it up to you, listen and reassure them. You can say something like, "Your mom is really angry right now and it sounds like she's having a hard time getting over it. I trust that she will get past it. The most important thing for you to know is that I love you and that she loves you—no matter what." If you're concerned that it's causing them stress, give them access to a therapist so they can share feelings in a neutral space.

What if you've already made one or more of these

mistakes? Use it as an opportunity to teach your kids how to apologize and make amends. In other words, own up to it with them. Tell them you're sorry about what you said, or have been saying to them, about their other parent. Tell them it is not okay and that you made a mistake. Tell them you were angry but now you know there are better, more constructive ways to deal with your anger. This teaches them what it looks like to gracefully take responsibility for your mistakes and to apologize. Then, do better. Show them you are reliable and are putting them first.

Co-Create Your New Normal

To kids, what happens during a divorce is completely out of their control. Major, abrupt changes can leave your children feeling insecure. Living arrangements are often just the beginning. My oldest daughter is the kind of kid that likes routines and for things to stay the same, so the changes that came with the divorce were particularly hard for her. As her dad moved out and we three girls downsized to smaller living quarters, she struggled with adjusting.

I knew intuitively that she needed something she could control, so I found ways for her to make or at least contribute to decisions that impacted her. I brought the girls with me to look at potential new homes. We each shared our pros and cons list for each place. Once we chose a place, I let my oldest pick the paint color for her room. She decided where to put her furniture and to cover her walls with posters. I let the girls take turns deciding what to make for dinner and I made what they picked, no matter what—this was the origin of our fondly remembered "Steak and Cake" Saturdays.

My younger daughter was very sad to leave our old house. Her grief mirrored my own. So, about a week before the scheduled move, the three of us discussed how to say goodbye to our old house. At the store later, she spied candle holders and colorful candles and knew instantly what she wanted to do. All during that last week, the three of us lit the candles and walked from room to room. In each room, we said thank you to the house and we each said a blessing for the new family moving in. This gave her a sense of closure and choosing the way we said our goodbyes gave her some of her power back.

As things progress, sit down with your kids and discuss what new routines and traditions you all want to try out. Like many in the ranks of the newly divorced, my client Brad went from seeing his kids daily to a few days a week and every other weekend. This was a difficult adjustment but one made easier after they discussed it together. He and his nine-year-old fraternal twins, Hailey and Jack, decided they wanted to grocery shop together each week and prepare their simple meals as a team. They also decided that, unless there was a special event, they would get their favorite takeout on their Friday nights together and play card games. Being in on the decisions that impacted their lives worked wonders on the kids' ability to adapt to their new, two-household lifestyle.

Get Busy Healing Yourself

Your kids' happiness and well-being corresponds strongly with your happiness and well-being. If you are emotionally healthy and resilient, you are better able to show up as a calm, loving and present parent for them. Work to transition from guilt and worry to the realization that you have a golden opportunity to teach your kids important life skills. Not everything works out the way you want it to, but everything is a lesson we can use to learn and grow. Knowing how to fall down and get back up again with grace, humor and self-love is invaluable.

> *Work to transition from guilt and worry to the realization that you have a golden opportunity to teach your kids important life skills. Not everything works out the way you want it to, but everything is a lesson we can use to learn and grow.*

Do everything you can to support yourself so you can fully embrace this experience for the benefit of your children.

SHIFTY ACTION STEP (SAS)

Here are some tools to help you deepen and integrate the Chapter 7 shift into your life:

♥ SAS 10: Meeting of the Hearts and Minds

Be intentional about staying connected and in close communication with your kids during your divorce and beyond. In our overstuffed lives, it's easy to let days pass without truly checking in on a meaningful level with each of our kids. These are all strategies that will strengthen your connection now and for years to come:

Listen with Your Whole Self: Being masters of multitasking, we often do two or more things at once, and we do almost everything while continuously checking our phones. One of the most important things you can do for your kids is to stop, look into their eyes and listen with focused attention while they are speaking to you. Listen to the words but also listen to the energy and emotions under the words. By putting your full attention on your child, you will make a true connection with him or her. You will feel the difference and so will your child. He or she will feel heard in a very deep way.

> *By putting your full attention on your child, you will make a true connection with him or her. You will feel the difference and so will your child. He or she will feel heard in a very deep way.*

Schedule Family Time: When possible, come together for family meals, even if it's just once a week. This provides a relaxed time for you to connect and share what's going on with each other. Brainstorm with your kids

115

to come up with ideas and then schedule weekly, bi-weekly or monthly family activities, such as game night, story circle night, craft day, discover-a-new-part-of-our-city day or whatever sounds fun to all of you. Regularly scheduled fun times unite you as a family and create wonderful memories even as you are navigating tough experiences.

Go on Dates with Your Kids: In their *Parenting From The Heart* workshop, Linda and Ty Hatfield suggest scheduling a one-on-one "date" with each of your kids at least once a month. Let your child choose the date and time and give them a choice of activities within your time and budget limits. This gives you a chance to connect individually with each of your kids.

Quick Lift

Here's a proactive step you can take to get some immediate relief as you work through your bigger shifts.

▪ *QL 7: What I Like About You*

Another great suggestion from Ty and Linda is to give love and support and show appreciation for each family member, including you, with an Appreciation Banquet. Here's how it works:

1. Form a circle and put the first family member in the center. If there are only two or three of you,

pick a special chair or spot for the first f
member to sit.

2. The featured family member goes first and says, "One thing I appreciate about myself is _____."

3. Then, each family member takes a turn telling the person, "What I appreciate about you is_____."

4. Next, another family member is featured and the process continues until everyone has had a turn.

According to Ty and Linda, Appreciation Banquets can be done anywhere, anytime, including in the car, at a restaurant or during a special event. After an Appreciation Banquet, you will feel very close to and connected with your kids.

Summary

Chapter 7 discussed the sixth shift, moving from guilt when it comes to your kids, to using your divorce as a way to strengthen your bonds with them and teach them resilience. The chapter talked about the do's and don'ts of parenting your kids through and beyond divorce and provided lots of practical ideas to help your kids adjust and thrive.

CHAPTER 8

Shift On: Your divorce is a life "Do-Over"

The word *divorce* is from a Latin word that means "to divert or to change course." I love that! That's the life do-over aspect of divorce. Your divorce, no matter how it came about, has flipped you out of your comfort zone. As long as you are out—and you're going to be uncomfortable anyway—you're invited to use the experience to rebuild your life the way you've always wanted.

Our lives flow by like a fast river current. We get caught up in it and we default to reacting to what's in front of us rather than proactively creating what we really want. We stick to our routines, even if we're not particularly happy with them. If you allow it to be, your divorce can be a catalyst for positive change.

It's a very exciting time because all bets are off. Someone (maybe you) tipped the table of your life over and now you are invited to consciously choose what you want to put back on it—what do you want to create next? What works for you in your life? What doesn't? How do you want to spend your life energy going forward? What have you always wanted to do? What do you want to stop doing? But first, let's cut right to why we are doing this work. I'm inviting you to consciously decide how you want to use your life.

> *With the higher stakes of the acknowledged limit of my time here on earth comes a greater sense of fearlessness and freedom.*

Part of what inspires me is to remember that how I spend my lifetime matters. *Spend* is the operative word here. We have a tendency to think of individual days, hours and minutes as expendable. When it became very clear that my 89-year-old grandmother was dying, I had one of those life-altering epiphanies. The reality hit that I, too, have a set number of days. I actually felt a little dizzy as the information landed deeply in my heart. Far from depressing or alarming, this insight was exciting. It motivated me to stop treating a normal day with all the excitement of finding a penny on the sidewalk.

With the higher stakes of the acknowledged limit of my time here on earth comes a greater sense of fearlessness and freedom. Who cares what other people think? So what if I fall flat on my face? I'm going to stay wide awake to my time limit and live in active gratitude for each breath. Now when I get up in the morning, I say to myself, "My life has an expiration date and this is one of my days." It prompts me to enjoy my today even as I go after my dreams for tomorrow, spend more time with people I love and find something to appreciate about every experience, even the DMV!

Here's what I want you to ask yourself:

- Am I "spending" my life in a way that has meaning and brings me joy?
- Do I wake up feeling grateful to jump into my day?
- If my life ended tomorrow, would I be satisfied with how I used it?

If you can't answer yes to all of these questions, you have an opportunity. If you choose, you can set yourself up for more joy, love and peace in your everyday life and make a plan to follow your dreams.

Taking Care of Future "You"

Your life right now is the culmination of actions and inactions that you've taken in the past—today is a result of past decisions. Today's "you" has tremendous power to change things for future "you" with every decision you make—doing things for yourself *now* takes care of you later.

Not only can you enjoy a moment for what it is but you can also enjoy stacking the deck for your future self.

We talked about our super powers of Awareness, Choice, Focus and Intention in Chapter 3. We will now apply all of those to the fifth super power: Inspired Action. I use the phrase inspired action to differentiate actions that are infused with your intentions for yourself versus default actions.

> ❝ *Inspired actions can shift even things you have to do into things you approach with inventiveness, gratitude and love.* ❞

Inspired actions can shift even things you *have* to do into things you approach with inventiveness, gratitude and love. When I first started working with Sarah, she was far from feeling any of those things about her situation. A struggling single mom with two small children, she felt stuck in a dead-end job, was uncertain about her future and was perpetually worried about making enough money to pay her monthly bills.

"How am I supposed to take care of 'future' me and feel joy in my life right now when today's me is barely staying afloat?" she lamented. We started small. She set her intention to find the joy in her current situation and to take simple but consistent actions that would put her in a better position. She became aware that her persistent state of worrying was impacting her ability to enjoy her four- and six-year-old boys. After a full day at work, it was all she could do to get them fed and cleaned up for bed each night.

She decided to set aside her worries for two hours a night so she could be mentally and emotionally present with her boys. During dinner, bath time and reading before bed, she really focused on the sights, smells and sensations of the nightly routine as well as the love and innate sense of fun that these two little guys effortlessly exuded. Rather than completely exhausting her as the nightly caretaking had in the past, most nights she found that surrendering to the task at hand left her with a sense of calm energy. She committed to herself to apply for one new job online each night after her boys went to bed. Then, she committed to doing something nice for herself, such as taking a hot bath or reading a good book before bed.

These small actions began to make a big difference. Instead of thinking of the nighttime routine as a chore, she truly began to look forward to it as an important time to connect with her boys. After a few months of applying for a different new job every night, she began to get interviews and, ultimately, landed a better job closer to home that paid more.

I Have a Dream

One amazing way of taking care of future you is to take some time to explore your bigger dreams for yourself. You may know exactly what you want to do, but you've stopped yourself because you don't think you can have it or do it. I always wanted to write a book and one day I decided to just start—one page at a time. You are reading the result! Or, you may not have a clear idea of what you would like to do with your life, you just know it isn't what you're doing now.

The great news is that, either way, this whole thing is a big science experiment. You can try something you think sounds interesting by taking a class on it, getting the scoop from someone who is already doing it and/or trying it as a side project. Or, you may want to jump in with both feet. Either way, you will end up with more information.

❝ The only thing you have to do is get in touch with what you want for your life (or what you think sounds interesting for now) and take one step in that direction. ❞

Many years ago, after a few years in a stressful sales job, I was beyond burned out, but I had no idea exactly what I wanted to do. Instead of focusing on a specific job or industry, I focused on other aspects that would make up my perfect job situation. I knew I wanted challenging and creative work that was well suited to my inherent people skills. I wanted to work with talented and passionate people and I wanted to grow as a writer.

Knowing just this much helped me recognize a great opportunity when I met the owner of a public relations agency, a well-respected author herself, looking to fill a position. It was a great fit for that time in my life and exposed me to a variety of people and professions that inspired me to pursue my emerging passion for writing and coaching.

The point is, there are no "shoulds" here—how this goes is completely up to you. We are in a mistake-free zone! Nothing can go wrong and whatever happens is perfect. The only thing you have to do is get in touch with what you want for your life (or what you think sounds interesting for now) and take one step in that direction. See what happens. Repeat.

Finding the Extraordinary in the Ordinary

There is great value in going for one or more of your dreams, which is not mutually exclusive with finding joy in your life as it is right now. Cultivating joy in your life is a decision you can make every minute of every day. So many times I hear people say, "I'll be happy when I lose some weight," "I'll be happy when I retire" or "I'll be happy when I fall in love again." What I like to remind myself when I fall into the "I'll be happy when..." trap is that I owe it to myself to love this moment for what it is.

> ❝If you reach for thoughts that make you feel good, you can be happier right now. On a day-to-day basis, the question is not, 'What would make me happy?' A better question is, 'What about this situation can I enjoy and appreciate right now?'❞

Joy and happiness are emotions. If you reach for thoughts that make you feel good, you can be happier right now. On a day-to-day basis, the question is not, "What would make me happy?" A better question is, "What about this situation can I enjoy and appreciate right now?"

We spend the majority of our time on the most mundane and ordinary things to keep life moving forward. We can tune into joy, no matter what we're doing, so that we transform work and even boring or unpleasant tasks with humor, creativity and love.

Paying my bills used to be an exercise in stress for me. As I wrote each check, I would gloomily watch my balance drop. One day, after setting my intention to find the joy in this dreaded process, I shifted into gratitude for having the funds to pay each bill and appreciation for the service I was getting.

As I wrote my utility bills, I would take a moment and marvel at the fact that I can flip a switch and get light or turn a faucet and get water. These are modern conveniences that would have been miracles to our ancestors. I would even feel a wave of thanks toward my credit card company for fronting me credit when I needed it. This simple shift transformed a stressful chore into an exercise in intentional happiness.

Even if you are not in a job or career that you love right now, you can find joy in small ways every day. It may be the joy of a work friendship you have or joy in the chance to use one of your talents. Cleaning the house or running errands can go from a necessary bore to time to enjoy an audio book, podcast or your favorite music.

It's worth thinking about how you can transform mundane, boring or unpleasant tasks in your life into opportunities for joy.

SHIFTY ACTION STEP (SAS)

Here are some tools to help you deepen and integrate the Chapter 8 shift into your life:

SAS 11: Inside-Out Goal Setting

Goals are like little doors that open us to much bigger possibilities for ourselves. Each represents a desire, and our desires are clues to what will make us feel the most alive. Inside-out goals are distinct from other types of goals in that they are lit up from the inside—you can feel the difference.

Inside-out goal setting is really about taking intentional steps in the present to create your life the way you want it in the future. Start a list of goals, big or small, long-term or short-term, that come to you. Don't edit yourself; just write them down and create a running list. Once you get something down to work with, compare it to the "Inside-Out Goal Test Questions" below and revise, adjust or discard as you see fit. Let yourself "blue sky" it here; even put down things that you think could never happen.

1. _____

2. _____

3. _____

4. _____

5. _____

Take each of the goals you wrote down and use these questions to measure their potential to add the maximum juice to your life. If the answer is "no" to one or more of these questions for a particular goal, rework it or consider releasing it:

1. **Does this goal light up my soul?** Goals must have enough juice to light that internal spark of exhilaration inside you. Even mundane goals can be put in their bigger context to see how they serve your life. (For example, creating a budget now means a Hawaiian vacation this summer.)
   ☐ Yes
   ☐ No

2. **Is this goal coming from the inside?** Goals that are born from what we should be doing according to someone else, or society, are anemic.
   ☐ Yes
   ☐ No

3. **Is this goal bite-sized or can it be broken down into bite-sized pieces?** Success builds momentum. It's important to break your goals into bite-sized and doable pieces.
   - ☐ Yes
   - ☐ No

4. **Is this goal measurable?** It's motivating to see tangible progress, so make sure you can track your success.
   - ☐ Yes
   - ☐ No

5. **Am I working toward something?** It's much more energizing to frame your goal in terms of things you want to approach rather than things you want to avoid. Think "organize my office so I'm more efficient and peaceful" rather than "clean up that mess."
   - ☐ Yes
   - ☐ No

Remember, not all goals are worth pursuing—even if they seem like no-brainers. To be worthy of your energy and focus, goals must create a result that makes you feel more alive in the moment and/or moves you closer to heartfelt dreams. When you make a goal, you are making an investment—your time is a limited resource, so your choice in how you will spend it is powerful.

Baby Steps

Once you've landed on one or two goals that, if met, would change your life for the better or move you closer to something you dearly want for yourself, write out a very simple plan that lays out the first three steps. Your plan should include the name of the goal, which includes the benefit of the goal, a brief description and just the first three steps. (Important note: Although you may be tempted, putting more than three steps can overwhelm you and stop you in your tracks.) For example:

Inside-Out Goal: Bedroom Haven

Brief Description: Transform my bedroom into a relaxing sanctuary that recharges me and makes me feel like I'm living in a resort.

First Three Steps:
1. Call Mom and set a date for her to come and help me clear out clutter.
2. Go to the paint store and choose some wall color samples.
3. Set a date with my best friend to go to Antique Row to pick out a unique wall hanging.

Once you complete the first three steps, plan out the next three steps and so on until you meet the goal. Now it's your turn!

Inside-Out Goal:

Brief Description: _____

_____

First Three Steps:

1. _____

2. _____

3. _____

Visit www.DebPurdy.com/resources for a PDF of an Inside-Out Goal Setting Guide.

Revisions are Part of the Process

If you set a goal that you don't complete, revisit the goal and adjust it or abandon it without judgment. Maybe you're not ready to have the outcome or it wasn't really a juicy goal for you. If you still want the outcome—get creative and revise the action steps to ones that work better for your life.

For example, I had a goal of creating a workshop which included a step of writing for eight hours each week. Most weeks, I did not make eight hours. In fact, most weeks, I didn't write at all. With my full-time job, there was no way I could realistically set aside that chunk of time and I was inconsistent at sprinkling the writing hours throughout the week. After a while, I realized this wasn't working at all. Not only that, when I did sit down to write, I felt guilty instead of inspired. That's not good! I checked in and confirmed that finishing the workshop was still very important to me.

So, I decided to adjust my goal down to a number that was a no-brainer. I set my goal for writing one hour a week, which was very doable. Not only that, most weeks I averaged 5 or 6 hours and I felt very successful. I found I had tremendous energy for writing when I was keeping my commitment to myself.

I have a client, a graphic designer, who wanted more clients and projects. She set a goal for herself to make 50 sales calls per week (10 a day) because she believed that's what small business owners are supposed to do. Hey, that's sounds doable; except, she hated doing it. It was an outside-in goal—something someone else said she should do. She abandoned that goal and got creative about other ways to build her business. Instead, she started a great blog that offered her readers valuable tips and insights and her business grew so big, she had to hire an assistant.

Bottom line is that it's okay to revise or even abandon a goal that's not working for you—without judgment!

SAS 12: From the Future with Love

A Danish philosopher named Søren Kierkegaard said, "life can only be understood backwards; but it must be lived forwards." To me, that means that when looking

back at life events from a distance, we get a [
that we did not have while in the thick of thi
means that things have a tendency to work out in the end.

Imagine that you could bend time and sit down to tea
with yourself at age 95. What would your older and no
doubt wiser self, who already knows how it all turned out,
say to you? Fill in the blanks from that perspective:

- I'm so happy that you had the courage to

  _____.

- Please let go of those bad feelings about

  _____.

  I realize now it didn't matter in the big picture.

- I'm most proud of you for

  _____.

- Please spend more time doing

  _____.

- Remember to always be grateful for

  _____.

- Never doubt that you are good enough, smart
  enough and talented enough to

  _____.

With this conversation in mind, make your bucket list. Fill it with things that would make your 95-year-old self happy that you did them. Include big things like hiking the Grand Canyon or learning to paint and heartfelt things like making sure your family and friends know how much you love them.

Prioritize your list and start on the top one right now!

Quick Lift

Here's a proactive step you can take to get some immediate relief as you work through your bigger shifts.

▪ *QL 8: Daydream Believer*

A fun way to energize yourself about your goals is to spend some time daydreaming about what it will be like when you meet them. Not only will that feel wonderful, but you can use it to spur you on if you lose focus. Once you can imagine a snippet from your future life, write it down in a short and inspiring paragraph. You'll know if you did it right if reading it makes you feel expanded and excited about meeting the goal. Here's one I wrote when my goal was to release weight:

I love getting dressed in the morning! Starting with my fun bra and panty set that shows off my curves. It's wonderful to open my closet and know that anything I put on will complement my lean, strong, healthy body. I slip on my favorite formfitting black dress and sandals. I look amazing. I feel amazing. I'm confident and beautiful and I can do anything.

Keep your daydream handy and read it every day. If it loses its juice, write another, better one. When you read it, embrace the feeling of having met the goal. This is a fun and powerful tool to keep you on track.

◼ QL 9: Kind Is the New Happy

Doing all we can to bring a little light to those we touch in our daily travels also increases our own happiness and feelings of well-being. In countless studies, kindness and generosity have been linked to greater life satisfaction, stronger relationships and better mental and physical health—generous people even live longer.

The happiness we derive from giving to others creates a positive feedback loop: The positive feelings inspire further generosity—which, in turn, fuels greater happiness. Here are a few easy ways you can build your kindness habit and increase your own happiness in the bargain:

- Listen and pay attention when someone is talking to you and look them in the eye without checking your cell phone.
- Clean up after yourself in public spaces.
- Smile at and make a friendly comment to people who serve you, such as sales clerks and baristas.
- Ask if you can help the next time you see someone who looks down, frustrated or overwhelmed.

- Be polite on the road—even with less-than-polite fellow drivers. We've all inadvertently cut someone off—give other drivers the benefit of the doubt.
- Call someone who has touched your life, let them know the positive impact they made and thank them.
- Send a handwritten thank-you note when someone gives you a gift or does you a favor.
- Bring a meal to a sick friend or new parents. Offer to pick up a few things from the grocery store or pharmacy.
- Send an e-mail to your boss at work acknowledging the contributions of a colleague.
- Go through your closets and garage and find useful items to donate.
- Find a volunteer opportunity in your community and commit to it.

These are just a few of the countless ways we can improve the lives we touch. Make your own list and commit to choosing some items to incorporate into your regular routine. You'll be glad you did.

Summary

Chapter 8 discussed the seventh shift, using your divorce as the catalyst to more joy in your life going forward. It talked about following your bigger dreams while finding the joy that's available in your daily life.

A Final Word

Some of the best advice I ever got was "Fake it until you feel it." If you act like what it would look like to be strong, smart and happy, guess what? The mere act of imagining yourself with those attributes (or whatever ones you're striving for), and acting accordingly, will help bring it about. So, don't wait. Even as you work through your "stuff" with this book and other resources, it's okay to go ahead and claim the results you want and start living them now. One day, you will realize that you are really there, without having to fake it.

I also want to acknowledge that this is a process. When I first went through this myself, I made significant shifts. But, because life doesn't stay static, I occasionally came back to the ideas and exercises I've laid out in this book when different life events triggered more grief or anger in me. Sometimes, when I went back to redo part of the work, the information "downloaded" into my life in a deeper, more significant way than it did the first time I saw it.

It's my hope that this book has given you tools you can review and reuse as needed to regain your equilibrium and achieve even deeper levels of healing.

I'm sending you love and light for the deepest level of healing and joy available to you! I honor and acknowledge you for taking part in this level of personal growth and introspection. It will not only benefit you, but everyone you touch throughout the rest of your life.

You've got this! I believe in you.

With Much Love,
Deb

About the Author

Deb Purdy is a transformation coach, speaker, workshop leader and author. She brings a balance of inspiration, creativity and practicality to her work helping people use divorce as a bridge to a better life. Lovingly accepting, Deb's passion is helping others to reframe challenges into opportunities for deeper compassion and joy.

Deb successfully transitioned out of her 10-year marriage and, in the process, created a collaborative and friendly relationship with her ex-husband, who she considers her co-parenting partner.

Her journey to consciously create her own life with awareness and live with joy and authenticity led her to study coaching and launch her coaching business in 2005.

Deb holds a Master's degree in Spiritual Psychology from the University of Santa Monica.

Deb's Intention Statement

I intend to offer my support to those who seek to use every experience to create lives they love that are full of joy, enthusiasm and prosperity. By doing so, I increase my own joy and prosperity and help increase the sum total of love, peace and kindness in the world.

Acknowledgments

I would like to thank my friends and family for all of their support and faith in me as I set out to realize my dream of writing this book. My BFF Julie Taylor, who is the best cheerleader a person can have, is unwavering in her belief in me and that is a great gift. I want to thank my brother, Jeff Purdy, and my dear friends, Diane Lofgren and Mary Castillo, for reading my manuscript and providing invaluable feedback, encouragement and advice. I'm grateful to my wonderful editor, Vicki Gibbs. Thanks also to my aunt, Cheryl Mays, for reading an early draft and giving me two thumbs up. And, thanks to Greg Schultz from Creative Shoebox, Inc., for rescuing the cover and making it amazing.

Finally, I would like to thank my ex-husband Ron. Our marriage and divorce was the laboratory for personal growth and insights I wouldn't have gained any other way. Without what I learned alongside Ron, this book would not have been possible.

Let's Stay Connected

Visit DebPurdy.com and sign up to receive more resources from Deb:

- **You'll receive an instant *FREE GIFT*!**

- **You'll be subscribed to Deb's blog, packed with useful tips and info to support you in creating your joyful life.**

- **You'll be the first to know about special promotions, upcoming live workshops, webinars and new offerings from Deb.**

You may also be interested in …

If you enjoyed this book and would like more on divorce recovery, you may be interested in *My Divorce Recovery Kit*, Deb's five-part e-course which includes video and PDF support materials. Available for instant download, the course will further support you in using your divorce as a launch pad to a life you love.

Visit DebPurdy.com to learn more.

Made in the USA
Middletown, DE
21 January 2018